The Hunger Crop

POVERTY
and the
SUGAR INDUSTRY

by Belinda Coote

First published 1987
© Oxfam 1987
ISBN 0 85598 081 8

Typeset by Marshment & White, Bradford on Avon
Published by Oxfam
274 Banbury Road
Oxford OX2 7DZ

ACKNOWLEDGEMENTS

First and foremost my thanks go to those whose lives depend on the sugar industry, especially in Jamaica, Brazil and the Philippines, for their help with the research for this book. I hope that it does some justice to the message that they wished to put across.

Whilst many people generously gave their time to help with the research, special thanks are due to Matthias Brown, Simon Harris, Margaret, Anne and Steve Hodges, Tony Hill, Tony Klouda, Horace Levi, Alan Matthews, Simon Maxwell, Reg McQuaid, Roger Plant, Frances Rubin, Tom Schuller and Christopher Stevens, some of whom also commented on earlier drafts.

Thanks also to the staff of the National Federation of Sugar Workers, and their volunteers (Negros), the Alternate Resource Center (Davao) and the Magdadaro Foundation (Bukidon), the Social Action Center (Jamaica), the National Sugar Corporation (Jamaica), the International Sugar Organisation, the International Commission for the Co-ordination of Solidarity Among Sugar Workers, the Commission of the European Community, Tate and Lyle, the Overseas Development Institute, the International Labour Organisation and the National Farmers Union for their expert advice and assistance.

Particular thanks go to my colleagues in Oxfam, both overseas and in the UK, who provided invaluable information, suggestions and comment.

Finally, my special thanks to Tom, for his patience.

Belinda Coote
April, 1987

Note: *To protect their identity, the names of individual sugar workers, whose stories are told in this book, have been changed.*

All photographs are by the author except where indicated.

Contents

Introduction

AT THE HEIGHT OF THE ETHIOPIAN FAMINE in 1985 Oxfam was alerted to the plight of several million other people who faced starvation, on the sugar producing island of Negros, in the Philippines.

Unlike the barren, drought-stricken images of Ethiopia during the famine, Negros, with its lush green fields fringed by tall coconut palms, gives every appearance of being rich and fertile. But the appearance of agricultural opulence turned out to be deceptive. Oxfam found itself funding a major relief operation to send food and medicines to the island.

Negros was as bereft of food as a drought-stricken desert. The hospital wards were full of severely malnourished children. Out in the villages people were scratching a living from the tiny, over-cultivated plots around their houses, or trying to grow food on the narrow stretches of land along the roadsides. Hunger was widespread because only a very few had work.

The reason for this was that sugar cane is almost the only crop grown on the island and nearly a quarter of a million sugar workers had been laid off work. Without employment they had no means of support, for themselves or their families.

Most of the sugar produced in the Philippines is exported to the United States. However, due to a switch from sugar to High Fructose Corn Syrup in many manufactured products the US no longer needed to import so much cane sugar. The Philippines' export market was substantially reduced and the sugar industry, which already faced considerable problems, was forced to cut back on production.

The suffering of people on Negros graphically illustrates the reason why Oxfam is publishing this report. The production and sale of primary commodities, such as sugar, tea, coffee and palm oil, provides the back-bone of many Third World economies. Yet the marketing, financing and processing of them is usually controlled by rich industrialised nations, such as Britain. It is an unequal exchange that leaves the Third World producers highly vulnerable to changes in market conditions and factors outside their control.

Yet sugar presents a special set of problems. In recent years cane producers from the South have found that they are in direct competition with European sugar beet and North American corn syrup. As a result of these developments traditional markets for cane sugar have contracted and

i

prices have fallen to a fraction of production costs. Hardest hit are the Third World poor.

Nearly 60% of the countries where Oxfam supports projects produce sugar for export. Half of these depend on sugar as a regular source of foreign exhange earnings. In some countries Oxfam has direct experience of working with sugar workers. In many the problems faced by cane cutters and other sugar workers are inseparable from those of the rural poor in general who suffer from landlessness, unemployment or low wages and lack basic amenities or access to services.

The Hunger Crop traces sugar as an export industry from its colonial beginnings as a slave crop in the 18th century to the present day. It shows how Third World producers first became dependent on exports to 'developed' country markets and how they have been hit by fluctuating prices as a result of Northern agricultural policies. To help clarify the Third World producers' predicament, it analyses the various trade agreements including the Sugar Protocol of the Lomé Convention and the International Sugar Agreement. It also looks critically at the overproduciton of European beet under the Common Agricultural Policy and the implications for Third World producers.

The book looks at some of the ways in which cane producers have attempted to overcome the crisis in the sugar industry through diversification, ethanol production and reducing their dependency on traditional markets. It concludes that there are no simple solutions, but that there are two inter-related problems. Both have to be addressed. The first is the cane producing countries' need to generate foreign exchange. The second, and Oxfam's primary concern, is the pressing need to alleviate rural poverty. This necessitates political commitment on the part of Third World governments to implement changes such as land reform. However, there is a great deal that 'developed' country governments could do to assist.

Europe needs to reduce its beet surplus as a first step to an International Sugar Agreement that can control world sugar prices. The United States should compensate cane exporters for the loss of its markets. Aid could be directed at programmes genuinely designed to promote rural development, such as land reform, and the burden of debt repayments could be eased by partially writing them off or lowering interest rates.

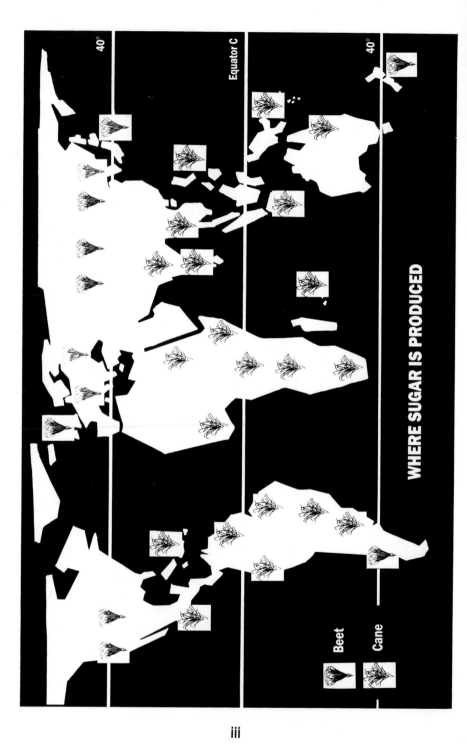

WHERE SUGAR IS PRODUCED

SUGAR

Sugar is derived from sucrose, a chemical substance which is present in all green plants. The most important sources of sucrose – in its processed form of sugar – are beet and cane.

60% of the world's sugar comes from cane and the rest from beet. It would be hard to imagine two more different plants and yet after processing and refining, the sugar produced from both is identical.

Whilst sugar cane, the grass, thrives in the heat and damp of tropical climates, sugar beet, the root, can only be grown in the world's temperate zones. This means first that sugar can be produced almost anywhere in the world and second that the vast majority of the world's sugar beet is grown in the 'First World' whilst most of its cane is grown in the 'Third World'. This makes sugar one of the few major agricultural commodities where the developed and developing worlds are in direct competition with one another.

Sugar cane is a perennial giant grass that belongs to the same plant group as maize and sorghum. It thrives in tropical or semi-tropical climates as it needs strong sunlight and abundant water.

The mature plant is 12 to 15 feet high with soft, sweet, juicy stalks that grow to a thickness of about two inches. It is propagated from cuttings of the stem which, once planted, mature quickly. This 'seed' cane will be ready to harvest in 11 to 18 months. After cutting, the remaining stubble will sprout again for the following year. The practice, known as 'ratooning' can be continued for 6 to 7 years or longer and is one of the economic advantages of cane over annual crops.

Much of the world's sugar cane is cut by hand. Just before cropping the leaves are often removed by controlled burning. Although this lowers the sucrose content of the cane it makes the harvesting much quicker and easier for the cutter. Cane cutting seasons usually last for 6 months of the year. For the rest of the time there is considerably less work involved in the production process.

Sugar cane deteriorates quickly when it has been cut and needs to be processed as soon as possible. Processing involves washing, shredding and crushing the cane. The cane extract is then soaked in water which is heated until the water evaporates and the sucrose becomes concentrated. As it cools it crystallises and emerges as 'raw' sugar. The by-products are molasses and bagasse, the residual fibre of the cane. The molasses is converted into rum, bakers' yeast and cattle feed. The bagasse is used mainly as fuel for the sugar factories.

The raw sugar still has to be refined before it becomes the product most familiar to consumers.

The tropical or sub-tropical regions where cane sugar is grown are climatically volatile. In any one year the grower is likely to face having the crop damaged by hurricane, cyclone, flooding, drought, pests or disease. Yet sugar cane is more resistant to adverse climatic conditions than many other tropical crops. The same wind that will destroy a crop of bananas may flatten a field of cane but it can still be harvested manually and will sprout up again the following year unharmed. As one geographer observed, "No other crop plant is so adapted to the ecological requirements of a humid tropical environment".[1]

Sugar beet is a root crop which can only be grown in the world's temperate zones. It is a favourite with many farmers because it is an excellent rotation crop and the whole plant can be used. Whilst its plump parsnip-shaped, sucrose-rich root can be dug up and sold for processing into sugar, its leafy green top, and the residue from processing, make good cattle feed. The seed is normally sown in the spring and the plant is harvested in the winter which is particularly welcome as green fodder is in short supply at that time of the year. Production is highly mechanised and farmers are generally well paid for their crop.

In Britain about half the sugar consumed comes from cane, imported from a number of African, Pacific and Caribbean countries, and the rest from home produced beet. Sugar that is sold by Tate and Lyle comes from cane, whilst sugar that is sold under the brand name Silver Spoon is beet sugar refined by the company, British Sugar . Other brands of packaged sugar may come from either beet or cane.

World Production of Sugar* – 1985
(Million Tonnes)

	TOTAL	BEET	CANE
WORLD	99.0	37.2	61.8
EUROPE	31.8	31.5	0.3
EC	13.5	13.2	0.3
USSR	8.6	8.6	—
ASIA	22.3	2.1	20.2
India	7.0	—	7.0
China	5.2	0.9	4.3
Thailand	2.4	—	2.4
CENTRAL AMERICA	14.5	—	14.5
CARIBBEAN AND CUBA	7.9	—	7.9
MEXICO	3.4	—	3.4
SOUTH AMERICA	13.5	0.4	13.1
BRAZIL	8.4	—	8.4
AFRICA	7.6	0.5	7.1
SOUTH AFRICA	2.5	—	2.5
NORTH AMERICA	5.5	2.7	2.8
USA	5.4	2.6	2.8
OCEANIA	3.8	—	3.8
AUSTRALIA	3.4	—	3.4

* Only those countries that produced 2.4 million tonnes or more are listed individually.
Source: SUGAR YEAR BOOK 1985. International Sugar Organisation.

Chapter 1

The Hunger Crop

Sugar plantation workers in Jamaica, the Philippines and Brazil

'Have to work so hard.
Have to work hungry.
Have children and rent house.
Me get seventeen dollars last week.
Can't drink tea
and we worked whole day in the sun.'

Jamaican sugar worker, Frome Estate, February 1986

Chapter 1

NELSETTA JOHNSON is one of 40,000 Jamaicans who earn their living from the island's sugar industry. Under the Sugar Protocol of the Lomé Convention Jamaica is entitled to sell some of its sugar to the European Community.[1] Each year it sends around 125,000 tonnes of raw cane sugar to Europe where it is refined at one of Tate and Lyle's refineries at Silvertown in London or Greenock in Scotland.

This trading arrangement is generally welcomed. It provides the Jamaican Government with a steady and reliable income as the price that the Community pays for its sugar is both fixed and set at a high level, unlike the world market price, which can fluctuate considerably but is generally depressed. For Tate and Lyle it means that there is a regular supply of sugar coming to their refineries which in turn ensures employment for several thousand people. It also means that Nelsetta Johnson is fortunate enough to have regular employment although under terms that are far from agreeable.[2] Hers is a life of plain hard labour and perpetual poverty.

Nelsetta works on Frome Estate, one of Jamaica's state owned sugar plantations. Situated in the parish of Westmoreland, at the western end of the island, the Estate is flanked by mountains to the north and west, and sea to the south and east. Frome factory, the hub of estate activity, sits among the cane fields pumping out black smoke when milling is in progress.

Since January 1985 both the estate and factory have been under the management of Tate and Lyle. The company is there on a ten year management contract, at the invitation of the Jamaican Government, as part of its strategy to revitalise the island's sugar industry. In Jamaica Tate and Lyle operate as the West Indies Sugar Company, known locally as WISCO.

Nelsetta lives in a small wooden hut in the middle of the estate. The house is provided rent free by the estate but has neither water nor electricity. She shares its one room with her two daughters, her three year old son and her mother, now retired after years of working in the cane fields. Like many women in Jamaica Nelsetta is head of her household.[3] The father of her children left home some years ago and has not been seen since. Some say that he has gone to work in the cane fields of Florida, others that he has joined the ranks of the unemployed in the ghettos of Kingston.

Nelsetta is one of a gang of six women field workers, assigned to tasks such as spreading fertiliser on the cane fields or planting cane. Each

Frome factory.

morning she rises before dawn to prepare breakfast for her children and food to take to work. She has to walk to work as there is no transport available. Depending on the cane field to which she is assigned this may be as far as six miles from her home. She has to be there by 7am when the factory siren signals the beginning of the working day.

When spreading fertiliser each woman has to provide her own plastic or wooden container. The fertiliser is brought to the fields in sacks, the containers are filled and for eight hours a day the women trek back and forth across the ploughed fields, scattering the fertiliser as they go.

They protect themselves from the burning sun and active ingredients of the fertiliser by putting on layer after layer of clothing. They are not provided with any protective clothing by the management even though some brands of fertiliser cause severe sores to their hands.[4]

At mid-day they break for an hour. A meal is prepared by two women assigned to that particular task for the day. It will consist of whatever the women have managed to bring with them from home – often very little and sometimes nothing at all. Frequently their lunch will consist only of boiled yams or green bananas, sometimes flour and water dumplings. They are usually joined by other work gangs and if they happen to be working in an area where no shelter is provided they sit eating in the heat of the mid-day sun.

3

Sugar workers' housing — Frome Estate.

The factory siren sounds the end of the day's shift at 4pm and the women return home, often complaining of hunger and exhaustion.

As a cultivator Nelsetta is paid the minimum agricultural wage of J$12.75 (£1.70) for an eight hour day. However, after deductions her take-home pay for a five day week is considerably less than her gross income of J$63.75 (£8.50). As illustrated in the pay slip (see figure 1) for one 40 hour week in January 1986 she took home just J$22.06 (£2.94), which means in effect that she worked for seven pence an hour. (Exchange rate Jan '86: J$7.50 = £1 sterling.)

Whilst all workers in Jamaica have money deducted at source for National Insurance, Income Tax and Government Bonds, Nelsetta, like many other workers on Frome Estate, opts to put J$10 (£1.33) into a credit union. This is her insurance against times of extreme financial hardship such as being laid off work, or to help her to meet unexpected extra costs such as funeral fees or hospital expenses. A further J$20 (£2.66) goes towards paying off a company loan and finally she pays union dues of J$1.20 (16p) a week.

After nearly forty years of work in the cane fields Nelsetta's mother receives a pension from the company of just J$15 (£2.00) a week. This brings their weekly joint disposable income to J$37.06 (£4.94).

But the cost of living is high. A group of nutritionists calculated the basic food needs for a family of five in Jamaica for one week. Their shopping list to meet these requirements would have cost J$175.37 (£23.38) in January 1986 (see chart), nearly five times the combined incomes of Nelsetta and

4

Spreading fertiliser, Jamaica.

her mother. The reality of this is that in order to buy one pound of rice Nelsetta has to work three hours eighteen minutes; to buy two pounds of sweet potatoes she must work four hours thirty-six minutes; and for one pound of spinach, two hours thirty-six minutes.

Some work on the estate is better paid. Factory workers, for example, earn J$15.45 (£2.06) a day, gross, whilst those employed to load or transport the cane receive an additional 34 cents a day (Figure 2; Frome worker pay slip 29.01.86 – trailer loader) As is so often the case in other countries and industries it is the jobs which are normally assigned to women – weeding, planting, fertilising – which are paid at the lowest rates. This leads to special hardships in Jamaica as many households there are headed by women. But even for those with the higher paid jobs in the sugar industry life is not easy. A foreman supervising cane cutting earns J$17.65 (£2.35) a day, gross. One Frome foreman worked seven eight-hour days in one week. His take home pay was J$134.17 (£17.89) (Figure 3) – still less than the estimated cost of feeding a family of five for a week.

All three pay slips (Figs 1, 2 and 3) were from a period when employment from the Jamaican sugar industry was at its peak. A particular cause of hardship is the cyclical nature of the industry.

January to June are the months when cane is being cut and employment is at its most plentiful. During this period Frome adds 1,000 cane cutters to its workforce. There is plenty of opportunity for overtime and weekend work. But for the rest of the year many people will be laid off work and a considerable number of regular employees will be put onto a three day working week with a corresponding reduction in their salaries. These are the lean months when hunger is a daily reality.

Cutting cane, Jamaica.

SUGAR WORKERS' WEEKLY PAY SLIPS —
FROME ESTATE, JAMAICA — JANUARY 1986

Fig 1 FOR SPREADING FERTILISER ON CANE FIELD (WOMAN)

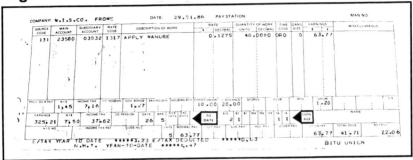

Net pay sterling equivalent £2.94

Fig 2 FOR LOADING CANE (MAN)

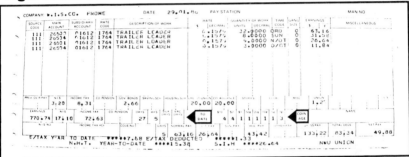

Net pay sterling equivalent £6.65

Fig 3 CUTTING CANE — FOREMAN (MAN)

Net pay sterling equivalent £17.89

Rate of exchange, end of February 1986 — 7.50 Jamaican dollars to each £1.00 sterling.

7

FOOD NEEDS FOR A FAMILY OF 5 FOR ONE WEEK

(Adapted from a survey carried out by the Caribbean Food and Nutrition Institute, University of the West Indies, Mona Campus, Kingston, Jamaica).

— Rate of exchange, end February 1986 — 7.50 Jamaican dollars to each £1 sterling.

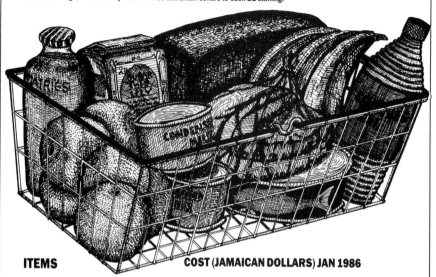

ITEMS — COST (JAMAICAN DOLLARS) JAN 1986

FRUIT AND VEGETABLES

6 lbs green bananas	3.30
4 lbs sweet potatoes	4.80
2 lbs dried peas	13.00
2 lbs pumpkin/carrot	2.40
2 lbs callaloo (spinach)	2.60
2 lbs cabbage	5.20
1 doz oranges	3.70
½ doz limes	0.50
½ doz ripe bananas	1.96
	37.46

CEREALS

6 lbs rice	10.50
6 lbs cornmeal	5.10
6 lbs flour	6.96
4 lbs bread	7.70
1 lb crackers	3.30
	33.56

MILK PRODUCTS

2 lbs skimmed milk powder	5.06
2 tins sweetened condensed milk	5.40
	10.46

MEAT AND FISH

5 lbs chicken necks and backs	12.50
½ lb salt fish	3.50
2 lbs pork (medium fat)	11.00
2 lbs canned mackerel	10.00
2 lbs tripe	11.90
1 lb minced beef	5.80
	54.70

FATS

1 quart cooking oil	14.09
2 lbs margarine	10.00
	24.09

SEASONING

6 lbs dark brown sugar	8.10
Spices, beverages, condiment	7.00
	15.10

TOTAL	**175.37**
	£23.38
	Sterling equivalent

8

FROME CULTURAL GROUP

Everyone suffers but it is the women workers – lower paid and frequently sole providers for a number of dependents – who suffer most. A number of women sugar workers from the Frome estate meet weekly to share their experiences. Originally assisted by a women's theatre group, SISTREN, from Kingston and supported by Oxfam, they express something of the way they feel about their lives and work through song, dance, poetry and theatre.

They call themselves the Frome Cultural Group and put together performances to entertain other workers around the estate. "It helps me to feel less alone," said one member of the group. "We are able to talk about our problems and this helps to make them easier and sometimes even solve them. Besides, I like to sing and dance and all those things. It makes me feel young again!"

HANDS

A poem put together by women sugar workers at Frome Estate during SISTREN workshop sessions.

Cracked hands, drop down hands,
Big hands, pain take over,
My hands are very stiff,
Rough hands, swell hands,
Working hands, nervous hands,
Hard working women.

My hands them corn up, sick and tired,
Dropping the fertiliser cause these hands to sore,
This work makes me hands them rough,
Them swell, them have arthritis,
Fingers them swizzle up,
Fingers them swell,
Through the hard work,
Fertiliser make them hands rough.

Old age take place with the hands,
Using to build them hands corn up,
Fingers them seize up,
Joints them numb and shaky,
Pressure cause that,
Years of exploitation take the poor two hands,
These hands do a lot of work,
These hands do a lot of work.

SISTREN is a Jamaican popular theatre collective of women which has been in existence for over a decade. The group formed during the 1970s as part of an extensive programme of social education facilitated by the Government of that period. Most of the women were originally street cleaners.

Frome cultural group.

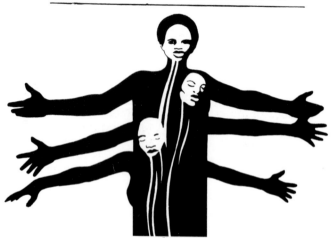

Women like Nelsetta survive because she is able to grow a few vegetables on a small plot of land behind her house. But she often goes to work hungry and can rarely afford to send her children to school. Most sugar workers need to combine subsistence farming with estate work in order to survive the chronically low rates of pay in the industry. The problem is that all the best land is taken up with sugar cane.

Jamaica is not the only country where Oxfam is involved in supporting programmes designed to assist sugar workers. In a number of areas where it works Oxfam has found sugar workers to be among the poorest and most oppressed sectors of society.

NEGROS

Oxfam has been concerned by the plight of sugar workers in the Philippines for many years. 68% of the country's sugar crop is grown on the island of Negros where much of the arable land is planted out to cane.[5] As a result Negros has to import most of its food from the other islands.

Unlike Jamaica the Philippines' sugar industry is privately owned. Many small farmers grow sugar as a cash crop on as little as half an acre of land but most of the sugar grown in the Philippines is owned and controlled by a small number of wealthy land-owners.

Their plantations are known by the Spanish term 'hacienda'. A typical hacienda in Negros is about 200 acres (some are much larger than this and some smaller). An estate of this size may support up to 50 families who would live on the **hacienda** in housing provided by the owner.

During harvest time additional labour is often needed. This is provided by seasonal migrant workers from other islands. Known as 'sacadas' (derived from the Spanish word 'sacar' literally 'to take out') they are the mainstay of the industry as they are crucial for harvesting the crop.[6]

Barrio Hagnaya

It takes about five hours to get to the tiny, remote village of Hagnaya from Bacolod, the capital city of Negros Occidental. First there is a bus trip along the coast road that leads to Escalante, scene of a massacre which took place in September 1985.[7] From there a jeepney, the local form of public transport, goes as far as the bottom of the rough half-mile track that leads up to the village.

About 40 families live in Hagnaya. It consists of 20 rudimentary bamboo houses each surrounded by a tiny plot of land. These were provided by the owner of the 234 acre **hacienda** as accommodation for his permanent workforce. He lives on a neighbouring island and last visited his **hacienda** in 1977. There is no electricity or running water in Hagnaya. Fields of sugar cane surround the village, stretching as far as the eye can see.

The workers of Barrio Hagnaya have been living in conditions of extreme poverty for as long as any of them can remember. In April 1986 they went on strike and constructed picket lines around the village. Inside the picket lines lay a number of trucks, vital to the work of the **hacienda**. As the workers explained, there is a higher premium on machinery than on their labour. If they allowed the trucks to be taken out of the village the managers of the hacienda would simply hire casual labour to work the cane fields. One thing there is no shortage of in Negros is labour.

Makeshift banners ranged across their picket lines telling something of the miserable conditions that they have to put up with. Their demands included the right to work an eight hour day – many of them had been put on a short working day and paid accordingly, causing considerable hardship to them and their families; wages consistent with the national minimum level – for some time they had been considerably lower; basic social security benefits – to which all Filipinos are entitled providing their employers make the correct contributions; access to a health clinic; the right to use idle cane lands for food production; equal pay for work done by men and women.

For the duration of the strike meals were being prepared communally with food donated by neighbouring **haciendas** where the workers were not striking at the time. The tiny plots of land around their houses were intensely cultivated with bananas, cassava, sweet potato and other food crops but there was only enough to take the edge off hunger.

Despite the additional hardships incurred through being on strike, morale was high. As one worker explained, "We have suffered for so long; either we fight for change or we watch our children become wasted from hunger with no hope for the future."[8]

Barrio Hagnaya — Striking sugar workers' picket line.

The workers from Barrio Hagnaya are not a special case. All over Negros workers are striking or speaking out against the conditions under which they have been forced to live for so long. They have suffered for years but only since the more liberal Aquino Government came to power have they been able to demand change without too much fear of a brutal military response.

During the strike meals were prepared communally.

13

BRAZIL

Brazil is one of the world's leading sugar producers. Of the eight to nine million tonnes that it produces annually about one third is exported and nearly half converted into alcohol-fuel for cars. Most of the industry is privately owned, but is state ocntrolled in respect of production levels, prices and subsidies. It provides direct employment for between three and four million people although about 40% of these are seasonal workers.[9]

In the North East of Brazil, where much of the country's cane is grown, around one million women, men and children work on the plantations. Sugar is known locally as 'the hunger crop'.[10] For a number of years, as part of its programme in NE Brazil, Oxfam has supported social, educational and legal aid projects to improve conditions for sugar workers. Despite annual campaigns to improve salaries, organised by the workers since 1979, conditions on the plantations and among the casual day labourers living on the edges of the rural towns, are deplorable.

The **Zona da Mata** is the name given to the humid coastal zone of the North East where sugar production is concentrated. The name originates from the Atlantic forest, the '**Mata**', that used to cover the region. Today very little remains. There are a few stretches on the hill tops and in some of the valleys that are too deep to plant cane.

A Cane Worker's Day

In the heart of the zone, about two hours drive from the state capital, Recife, the sound of a huge Mercedes truck shatters the pre-dawn silence of a small town. Joana wakes up with a sigh, wondering whether they will have a safe driver in charge of the truck that will take her and tens of other '**clandestinos**', the name given to the casual day labourers, to the plantations. Two years ago she lost her job on the local plantation because she stood as one of the unsuccessful opposition candidates in the local union election. She was forced to move out of her terraced house on the plantation, into the town to a small house which she shares with her five daughters, mother and husband.

Sometimes there is no work available but today Joana is lucky. The cane cutting season is at its height so work is plentiful. By 5am she has found a contractor who agrees to take her on. she is assigned to work that involves clearing the land in preparation for planting. For an exhausting day of hard, physical work, she is paid 60 cruzados (£2.12), which is calculated by the area that she has managed to clear.[11] It has been a good day for her as she feels physically fit. Some of the older workers only managed to clear enough to earn half of that amount. As the plantation is a considerable distance from her home she doesn't arrive back until late in the evening.

Joana's husband, Carlos, has a full time job on a nearby plantation. When cutting cane he can earn between 200 and 300 cruzados a day, depending on the weight of the cane that he manages to harvest. When there is no cane to cut and only planting, weeding or fertilising work available, he earns much less. On their combined income Joana and Carlos can just about manage to

Frances Rubin

keep their family fed. Each week they buy manioc, beans, sugar, maize meal, rice, eggs, and some coffee. They estimate that it takes them about one or two hours work to earn enough to buy a packet of sugar.

Plantation Life

Life is not much easier for those who live on the plantations. Lucia and her family live in a house that is typical of workers' dwellings on many of the plantations. They are one of ten families who live in a terrace of small houses constructed out of brick and wattle and daub. The 'cabo' (or foreman) lives at one end. He measures the area of cane to be cut, or rows to be cleared. Generally it is a good idea to keep on the right side of him.

There is no electricity or running water. Water has to be fetched from over the road where a well has been sited in the middle of a cane field. The only place for washing and bathing is a muddy stream about a quarter of a mile away.

Frances Rubin

At the back of the terrace the families have planted manioc and beans, and a variety of fruit trees. Little by little they have been extending into the cane fields but the bailiff has warned them not to go any further. They take his warning seriously. In a neighbouring settlement a goat was recently shot as it drank by a stream, as a warning to the workers not to raise livestock.

Frances Rubin

17

Lucia, three of her six children, and her husband, all work on the plantation. Yet with their combined pay often they cannot even afford to buy basic food items. The main food that the family eats is manioc flour. When there is not much work on the plantation and income is low this is simply mixed with water, or even a bit of cane juice. They often go hungry.

A nutrition survey carried out in the **Zona de Mata** in the 1960s found many of the cane workers to be malnourished due to a low intake of essential foods.[12] The researcher found that many of the workers left home in the mornings without having eaten. He calculated that the average cane worker has a daily intake of 1,500 calories, less than half the amount needed for such physically demanding work.[13] A more recent survey concluded that 80% of workers' income is spent on food.[14] Nowadays, with payment equalling around seven to twelve pence an hour, depending on an individual's productivity, this may be even higher.

One consequence of the difficulties workers face in earning enough to be able to survive, is a high illiteracy rate. As children often have to help their parents out, either by working in the cane fields, or by taking responsibility for the household, many miss the opportunity to attend school. Lucia's two eldest girls, aged 14 and 15, and their 11 year old brother work with their father cutting cane in the harvest season. They fit in seven or eight hours work in the morning, help in the house in the afternoon, and then go to school at 7.30pm. Luckily for them they live within easy reach of the town. For those in more remote areas attending school is even more difficult.

Figures for the municipality of Sao Lorenzo da Mata, a typical town in the cane zone, show 43% of the population as illiterate. However, the problem of illiteracy is probably greater as less than half of the more literate had more than four years of primary education.[15] As Oxfam project partners often stress literacy is not just a question of being able to read and write. It is crucial to people beginning to gain control over their lives and the lives of their communities, campaigning for better wages and conditions.

There are about twelve million people employed in Third World cane sugar production. Not all of them are employed on plantations. In some parts of the world, such as Fiji, sugar is grown by small farmers who sell their crop harvest to the factories. Small farmer production co-exists with plantation production in Jamaica and the Philippines whilst in Peru and Cuba sugar is grown by cooperatives.

Whilst all sugar workers are vulnerable to periods of low income when the price of sugar falls, conditions on plantations tend to be particularly bad as workers rarely have access to land where they can grow food. The plantation system is as old as the industry itself. Sugar plantations have been in existence in Jamaica, for example, for several hundred years and still the workers live in poverty.

Chapter 2

King Sugar

The history of the
cane sugar industry

'The sweetening of the British tea
has always taken priority over the filling
of the Jamaican stomach.'

Joe Owens — Jamaican Sugar Worker organiser.

Chapter 2

IN APRIL 1986 representatives from sugar workers' organisations around the Asia-Pacific region gathered for a meeting on the island of Negros.[1] It was an opportunity for delegates to share the problems that workers in the industry in their respective countries face and discuss ways in which these problems could be overcome.

Each delegate had a story to tell. From India we heard of an attempt by cane cutters in one region to secure basic medical and educational facilities and of an explosion in an ethanol factory that killed 12 people and seriously injured many more.[2] From Thailand we heard how many of the country's 120,000 sugar cane farmers are crippled by debts due to the high interest charged on loans for inputs. From Indonesia we heard how farmers, encouraged to grow sugar instead of food crops in a national drive to increase sugar production, had suffered when there was a crop failure after a drought in 1983. In Sri Lanka farmers are being driven off their lands to make way for a huge sugar cane plantation.[3] In the Philippines, a crisis in the sugar industry, has laid off thousands of sugar workers on the island of Negros, leading to widespread poverty and starvation.

Whilst sugar workers from each country faced their own special set of problems a depressing picture of poverty and deprivation emerged. Yet each delegate acknowledged the importance of sugar to their country. Besides its potential to provide employment, many developing countries depend a great deal on sugar as a source of foreign exchange. To understand how this dependency came about and why so many sugar workers live in poverty it is helpful to look at the growth and evolution of the industry – back to the days when sugar was 'King' during the colonial period and era of slavery.

Sugar cane is a native of Polynesia where it was once invested with near magical properties. This arose, perhaps, from the fact that small pieces were often found washed up on foreign shores where they inevitably flourished, and probably explains how sugar cane came to be found in China, India, the Philippines and elsewhere. It was reported to have been first refined into sugar in India around 700BC.

Sugar cane and its production into sugar were established in the Mediterranean region around 1000AD. Some speculate that its introduction to the region followed Mohammed's banning of alcohol to his followers. At first, alternative stimulating drinks had to rely on honey for sweetness but soon after the Prophet's death in 632AD it was replaced by the more plentiful, accessible sugar from cane.[4]

Once in the Mediterranean sugar soon found its way to Europe. It first arrived in England in 1319 but for many years was just an expensive novelty.

Over the course of the next 200 years the price of both sugar and honey declined – probably due to increased production of cane sugar in areas outside the Mediterranean. Recognising the market potential of sugar in Western Europe, the Portuguese had planted cane in Madeira, the Spanish planted it in the Canaries and in 1493 Christopher Columbus had introduced sugar cane to the Caribbean on his second voyage to Hispaniola, the island now divided into the Dominican Republic and Haiti.[5]

Sugar cane thrived in the fertile soils and semi-tropical climate of the West Indies. The first recorded sugar mill in the region began grinding in 1516 in what is now the Dominican Republic. Before the end of the 16th century sugar was also being produced in Cuba, Jamaica, and Puerto Rico, all then under Spanish rule.

In the course of the following century British, Dutch, French and Danish settlers planted cane and built sugar mills on more than a dozen islands of the Eastern Caribbean. The centre of the world's sugar industry had shifted from the Mediterranean and East Atlantic islands of Madeira and the Canaries to the West Indies region which, by 1800, was responsible for producing more than 80% of the world's sugar – and for more than 80% of the world's trade in slaves.[6]

COLONIALISM AND SLAVERY

The history of sugar production is inextricably mixed with that of colonialism and slavery. The work involved in its cultivation has always been dirty, hard, repetitious and labour-intensive whilst processing involves long hours in high temperatures and humidity as the liquids are boiled and cooled.

The European settlers in the West Indies were neither willing nor able to do all the work required to produce sugar. The indigenous peoples of the islands that they had colonised had either died, fled or retreated to the interior to wage war on their colonisers – so the settlers turned to the slave trade for their workforce.

As a result the Caribbean became Africanised. Between 1450 and 1900, 11.7 million captured West Africans were imported to the Caribbean. Just under 10 million reached their destination alive and were sold as slaves to work the plantations. They were one leg of a profitable triangular trade which went from England to West Africa with trinkets, cloth, firearms and salt to be traded for Africans destined to the Caribbean plantations, who in turn were exchanged for raw sugar and rum destined for the small refineries in England. Due to the harshness and cruelty of their existence many slaves died. In 1800 it was estimated that, in that year, for every two tonnes of sugar imported into England, one slave had died.[7]

21

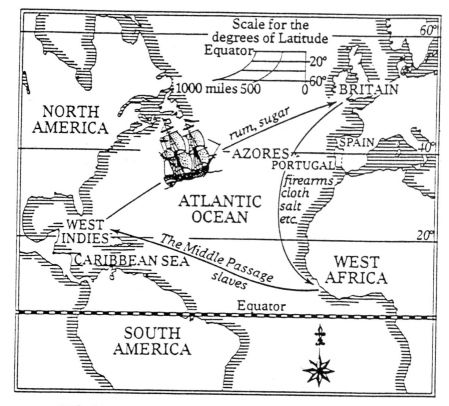

The Triangular Trade

Seeds of Change by Henry Hobhouse   Sidgwick and Jackson (1985)

Milne Stebbing Illustration.

Britain played a key role in the slave trade. Its sugar industry began in Barbados when the first sugar factory in the British 'New World' colonies was built in 1641. Forty years later there were more than 46,000 slaves working on the sugar plantations in Barbados. In turn other British colonies, Antigua, St Kitts and Nevis became slave worked sugar islands. By the next century Jamaica had become the most important source of sugar in the British Empire.

The sugar was imported in a semi-refined state to be further processed in Britain. This practice was encouraged by a tax imposed in 1670 on all imported refined sugar. The effect of this tax was not only to make the colonies dependent on the mother country, but it also led to the establishment of the British sugar refining industry.[8]

After about 1680 one of the quickest ways to fortune in Britain was through the triangular trade. The mercantile class prospered as the trade grew into a vast industry involving several hundred ships. Sugar made Bristol the second largest city and seaport in England until the middle of the 18th century when it was surpassed by Liverpool.[9]

The triangular trade stimulated considerable industrial development. Shipbuilding expanded as a direct result as did the manufacturing of household utensils, cloth, iron and other metals, guns, handcuffs and fetters. This expansion required capital so the banking and insurance industries also prospered. By the mid-18th century sugar was said to be supporting "half Lancashire and a quarter of all British shipping."

When sugar was first introduced into England in the 14th century it was classified as a spice, but used mostly for medicinal purposes. By the 16th century, when production had expanded from the Mediterranean to include the East Atlantic coast islands it had started to be used as a preservative. It was also being used in some recipes, but mainly for decoration.

The introduction of tea, coffee and chocolate into Europe did much to boost demand for sugar and greatly encouraged the expansion of the Caribbean industry. From around 1680 these hot drinks became fashionable. All three, it was said, were undrinkable without sugar and consumption rose from 4lb per head in 1700 to 18lb in 1800.[10]

Sugar was eventually established as a common food in England in the 1800s when the temperance movement advocated sugared tea as a respectable alternative to alcohol and dessert became an accepted part of the mid-day or evening meal. The tarts, buns, pies, pastries, biscuits, cakes and puddings that turned up more and more in the English diet after 1750 and in a deluge after 1850 meant that sugar partly supplanted the consumption of bread and flour, which had become relatively more expensive. It was rapidly becoming the quickest, cheapest, most palatable source of energy available and was the single most important addition to the British diet during the 19th century. By 1900 it was contributing nearly one sixth of the calorie intake per person and by 1960 average consumption was 120lb per head.[11]

While consumption was increasing, the way in which sugar was being produced began to cause concern which gave rise to the anti-slavery movement. Perhaps the most famous of reformers was William Wilberforce. He spoke in Parliament on behalf of the Society for the Abolition of the Slave Trade, founded in 1787, and fought against slavery steadily for 40 years. John Wesley was also a strong abolitionist, preaching powerful sermons against slavery.

The British Government passed an Act in 1807 which legislated against the transport of slaves, but the use of slave labour continued for nearly 30 years until the Emancipation Act of 1833.

Beneficiaries of the sugar industry in the West Indies said that the industry could not survive without slavery. In 1838 a quarter of the world's sugar supplies came from the British Caribbean colonies. However, the decline of the industry in the second half of the 19th century was as much due to the increased production of European sugar beet as to the abolition of slavery.[12]

$150 REWARD

RANAWAY from the subscriber, on the night of the 2d instant, a negro man, who calls himself *Henry May*, about **22** years old, **5** feet **6** or **8** inches high, ordinary color, rather chunky built, bushy head, and has it divided mostly on one side, and keeps it very nicely combed; has been raised in the house, and is a first rate dining-room servant, and was in a tavern in Louisville for **18** months. I expect he is now in Louisville trying to make his escape to a free state, (in all probability to Cincinnati, Ohio.) Perhaps he may try to get employment on a steamboat. He is a good cook, and is handy in any capacity as a house servant. Had on when he left, a dark cassinett coatee, and dark striped cassinett pantaloons, new---he had other clothing. I will give **$50** reward if taken in Louisvill; **100** dollars if taken one hundred miles from Louisville in this State, and **150** dollars if taken out of this State, and delivered to me, or secured in any jail so that I can get him again.   **WILLIAM BURKE.**

Bardstown, Ky., September 3d, **1838.**

SLAVES AT SALE,
WITHOUT RESERVE.
BY BEARD, CALHOUN & CO.
J. A. BEARD, Auctioneer.

WILL BE SOLD AT AUCTION ON

Tuesday, Jan. 16th,

AT 12 O'CLOCK, AT BANKS' ARCADE, THE FOLLOWING DESCRIBED NEGROES:

1. **ROSIN,** 13 years of age a griffe, good house boy, fine temper, fully guaranteed, and speaks German and English.
2. **JORDAN,** 23 years of age, a likely negro, house servant and trusty waiter—fully guaranteed.
3. **JANE,** aged 24 years, a very superior washer, ironer, good American cook and house woman—fully guaranteed.
4. **MARY,** aged 24 years and child 1 year old, a trusty woman, good washer, ironer and American cook—fully guaranteed.
5. **EDWIN,** aged 27 years, a griffe man, an excellent waiter, steward, and trusty servant—fully guaranteed.
6. **ESTHER,** aged 40 years, a smart intelligent and cleanly cook, washer and ironer—title only guaranteed.
7. **ANNE,** aged 24 years, an excellent house servant, washer, ironer, and good cook, with her three children, one aged 5, another 2 and the last 1 year; they are fully guaranteed, but will be sold to go into the country, by her owners instructions.

8. **SAM,** aged 28 years, a field hand; title only guaranteed.
9. **AGNES,** aged 24 years, a good cook, washer and ironer—fully guaranteed.
10. **HENRY,** aged about 26 years, a field hand, and a stout man, sold as having ran away from the plantation.
11. **JOHN,** aged 15 years, a smart waiting boy—fully guaranteed.
12. **JANE,** aged 17 years, a fine house girl and field hand—fully guaranteed.
13. **MARY,** aged 35 years, a superior nurse and house woman—fully guaranteed.

ALSO:

14. **PATRICK,** aged 28 years, a likely man, good barber, body and house servant. Sold under a good character, and fully guaranteed against the vices and maladies prescribed by law.

TERMS CASH. Acts of sale before J. R. BEARD, Notary Public at the expense of the purchasers.

ALSO,

The following described Slaves sold for account of Mr. Henry Deacon, who failed to comply with the terms of sale made for the account of the Succession of C. H. L. ELWYN, deceased, to wit:
The Negress **MATHILDA,** aged about 29 years and her son **PAUL,** 7 years--a good washer, Ironer and Cook.

TERMS CASH. Act of Sale before H. B. CENAS, Notary Public, at the expense of the Purchasers.

Celina de Godoy

Satisfying the European and North American sweet tooth involved the creation of a massive industry throughout the tropical or sub-tropical regions around the world. While the economies of Europe and North America forged ahead as they built refineries, factories, ships and railways, the colonies remained geared to the production of primary commodities – including sugar. Workers were not paid at all if they were slaves, or very little if they were free labourers. Local industries had difficulty in developing because the vast majority of the population had no money to spend.

When independence came to many Third World countries in the 20th century their position in the world economic system had already been set. They lacked the finance and the necessary technological expertise to carry through industrialisation programmes. Health and education improvements were essential to provide a solid base for development but they soaked up scarce resources.

Developing countries had to continue to produce sugar and other primary commodities for export because that was what they were geared up to produce and it was the only means they had of accumulating precious foreign exchange. Production costs had to be kept to a minimum because of stiff competition from other exporting nations, which is one reason why wages have remained low.[13]

Many Third World countries, whose industries were developed under colonial rule, remain dependent on sugar as a source of foreign exchange. This is illustrated by the parallel experience of three very different countries, Jamaica, Mauritius and the Philippines.

USA

MEXICO

CUBA

HAITI

DOMINICAN REPUBLIC

JAMAICA

CARIBBEAN
SEA

VENEZUELA

JAMAICA

Jamaica's sugar industry was developed under British colonial rule in the last quarter of the 17th century. Having been 'discovered' by Columbus in 1494 and settled by the Spanish a few years later the indigenous population had been decimated by the time Britain colonised the island in 1655. The few that remained settled in the interior of the island and waged constant warfare on the British settlers.

Aware of a growing demand for sugar in Britain the settlers brought in high quality sugar cane from Barbados and began to transform their small family farms into large plantations with the labour of slaves imported from West Africa. The industry flourished and by the end of the 18th century Jamaica had become the centre of the West Indies sugar trade.[14]

Widespread disaffection among the Jamaican slaves led to protests and rebellion and the planters had to employ British troops in order to maintain slave society. After emancipation in 1838 many of the slaves fled the plantations and the industry fell into disarray. Production declined and by the end of the 19th century the industry had all but collapsed.

It revived during the first half of the 20th century. The destruction of the European sugar beet industry during the first World War meant that markets for cane improved. This attracted foreign investment to the island.

In 1928 the American-owned United Fruit Company took over three factories. Ten years later the West Indies Sugar Company (WISCO) a wholly-owned subsidiary of the British company, Tate and Lyle, had purchased two plantations and built a large factory. They continued to expand operations and were joined by other companies until, by the end of the 1960s, two thirds of Jamaican sugar was controlled by foreign interests, principally WISCO.[15]

The signing of the Commonwealth Sugar Agreement in 1951 assured Jamaican sugar continued access to the British market. With renewed confidence in their export market the companies expanded operations and production increased dramatically.

But the gains were to be shortlived. Increased production was due to increased acreage, not improved efficiency. In the drive for expansion and quick returns nothing was done to improve technology or sugar yields. After production peaked in 1965 the industry went into decline and soon became inefficient and costly.[16] As cane yields fell and factory breakdowns reached crisis porportions both Tate and Lyle and United Fruit sold their interests to the Jamaican Government.

In 1972, following a change in government, the plantations were placed under the management of workers cooperatives.[17] However, production continued to decline and eventually the cooperatives were dissolved. The old-style plantation system was re-introduced and Tate and Lyle were invited back by the Government to manage the industry in 1985.

Jamaica continues to export most of its sugar to Britain under the Sugar Protocol of the Lomé Convention.[18] Despite the problems that the industry faces sugar has continued to be an important source of foreign exchange, contributing about 8% of earnings in 1985. Sugar is also socially and politically important to Jamaica as more than a quarter of its working population earn their living from the industry.

27

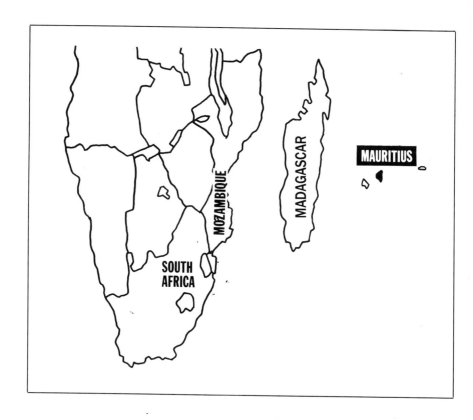

MAURITIUS

It was the Dutch who first introduced sugar to Mauritius, but the French who developed the industry when they colonised the island in 1721 and imported African slave labour to work on the plantations. In 1815 Mauritius became part of the British Empire. With slavery abolished the British brought in indentured labour from India to do the backbreaking cane cutting and to work in the growing number of sugar mills. In 1968 Mauritius became independent but its dependence on sugar remains entrenched.

Situated in the Indian Ocean, with a population of less than one million, 65% of Mauritius' foreign exchange earnings come from sugar. At one time it was a great deal more than this but the development of other industries, such as textiles, tea and tourism, have helped to lessen such a massive dependency on one crop.

Mauritius has failed to diversify more fully out of sugar because it is one of the very few crops that can withstand the cyclonic weather conditions that prevail on the island.[19] As a result 90% of Mauritians are dependent on sugar for a livelihood which makes it of central concern to the islanders.

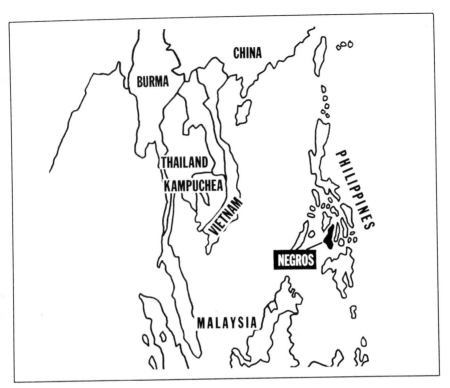

THE PHILIPPINES

Sugar was grown as a subsistence crop in the Philippines long before it was grown for export. It was a British coloniser, Nicholas Loney, who saw its potential as an export crop and brought in a shipment of machinery for sugar production in the 1850s. Shortly afterwards, the industry entered the world market and sugar accounted for 33% of the country's export earnings. Since then, due to an expansion in other export industries, such as copra and tropical fruits, sugar has declined in relative importance to the Philippines' economy but still makes up 8% of foreign exchange earnings.[20]

The principal market for Philippines' sugar has traditionally been the United States which has increased or decreased imports according to its own market requirements.

The Philippines was still under Spanish colonial rule when it began to export sugar to the United States. Since then the fortunes of the industry have rested almost entirely on the US which has controlled the flow of Philippine sugar imports through a series of trade agreements.

In 1898 the United States colonised the Philippines and lifted all restrictions on trade between the two countries. It encouraged increased production of sugar to meet a steadily growing consumer demand.

However, as farmers in the United States began to increase their own

29

production of sugar, in 1934 the US established a quota system to regulate imports. For the Philippines this meant that its raw sugar exports at a guaranteed price were restricted to 800,000 tonnes a year.

In the course of the next thirty years this quota was progressively reduced. However, following the Cuban revolution in 1959 the United States stopped importing sugar from Cuba, which had been one of its main suppliers.[21] The Philippines was asked to fill Cuba's sugar quota and as a result extended its sugar lands and intensified cultivation.[22]

As US domestic sugar production increased during the 1970s there was less need for it to import so much sugar from the Philippines. Subsequent-cut backs on imports have meant that by 1986 only 231,000 tonnes of Philippines sugar, one quarter of the 1930s level, were destined for the US market. Further reductions are expected over the next few years.

In the Philippines it costs approximately 12 US cents to produce each pound of sugar. For the sugar that it sells to the US it is paid the support price of 21 US cents per pound. As it has been gradually squeezed out of the US market, the Philippines has had to look to the world market to sell increasing amounts of its sugar. However, the world market price for sugar has crashed from a high of 28.66 US cents per pound in 1980 to 3.51 cents per pound in December 1984. This is way below its production cost and has led to a major reduction in income from its sugar exports.

Such reduced income from exports has meant that many of the country's sugar planters are unable to meet their production costs. As a result, in the crop year 1984 to 1985, only half the area planted to sugar on the island of Negros was harvested, and a quarter of a million people found themselves without work or means to provide for themselves or their families.

The tiny plots beside their houses are the only land available for sugar workers to grow food crops.

WHO EATS THE WORLD'S SUGAR

Every year approximately 96 million tonnes of beet and cane sugar are consumed worldwide at an average rate of 20.3 kilos per person. There are, of course, substantial regional variations. Top of the league is Cuba whose population got through an average of 65.3 kilos per person in 1985, whilst the Kampucheans only consumed an average of 0.7 kilos per person, in that year. (Sugar Year Book 1985)

The biggest consumers of sugar have historically been those industrialised nations which colonised sugar producing countries and developed their own export markets. Now, however, in the same way as sugar consumption shifted from the wealthy to the poor in Britain during the 18th and 19th centuries, the bulk of sugar consumption is gradually shifting away from the richer industrialised nations to the poorer industrialising Third World countries. The figures show that whilst in some developed countries there has been a dramatic reduction in consumption over the last decade in many Third World countries consumption has risen.

Levels of consumption per capita of white sugar, (raw value) kilogrammes – in selected countries:

Developed country sugar consumption.	1974	1985
EC	45.1	38.4
USA	48.0	30.5
Japan	30.4	23.9
Australia	57.3	48.5

Third World country sugar consumption.		
India	6.5	12.0
Jordan	19.1	43.5
Egypt	17.0	33.3
Zimbabwe	20.5	27.3
Mexico	40.3	45.3

Source: Sugar Year Book 1985 and 1977

Projections for 1990 are that there will be a 2.2% increase in world consumption. As the following table shows this the increases in consumption will be in developing countries and will offset a corresponding decrease in consumption in developed countries.

Projected sugar consumption to 1990, showing percentage annual growth 1979/80 to 1990

WORLD	+2.2%		
DEVELOPED	**−2.0**	**DEVELOPING**	**+4.2**
North America	−2.0	Africa	+3.4
Western Europe	0.0	Latin America	+2.7
Eastern Europe	+0.8	Near East	+3.2
		Asia	+6.0

Source: FAO Economic and Social Development Paper, 50, (1985) Sugar: major trade and stabilisation issues in the eighties. Table 8.

The Cane Trade

How sugar is traded around the world

'No nation was ever ruined by trade.'

Benjamin Franklin (1706 — 1790) *Thoughts on Commercial Subjects*

Chapter 3

IN MAY 1986 JENNIE ANNAS celebrated her second birthday in the malnutrition ward of Bacolod City hospital, Negros. Her story was typical of many of the children on the ward.

Mr Annas was a sugar worker on one of Negros's **haciendas**. Towards the end of 1984, not long after Jennie was born, the owner of the **hacienda** decided to cut down on the scale of his operations as he was no longer able to get a good price for his sugar. With the milling season due to start in October his workers were looking forward to a period of full employment after a lean three months during the annual 'dead season' when the only jobs available on the **hacienda** are weeding and fertiliser application. His decision to leave half of his cane fields either unharvested, or fallow, was greeted with dismay. Mr Annas found that he only had work for three days a week instead of the five he had expected.

The Annas family scraped by. With four children to feed they found it difficult to buy enough of even the most basic foods. But by supplementing their rice with the few vegetables they were able to grow on the small plot of land by their house they found they could generally have one good meal a day.

By February 1985, three months earlier than usual, the cane was all harvested and the milling season at an end. The workers faced a 'dead season' of six or seven months instead of the usual three. Mr Annas found himself without work or pay. The only family member who was able to find occasional work was his ten year old son. For picking thatch out of harvested, unmilled cane, he was paid twelve pesos (about 40p) a day, just enough to keep the family in rice – but at the expense of his schooling.

Mrs Annas became ill. Lack of nutritious food combined with the worry of feeding her family meant that her milk supply gradually dwindled and very soon she was no longer able to breastfeed the baby, Jennie. Deeply in debt to the local stores the Annas found it increasingly difficult to get food on credit. Jennie was losing weight rapidly and soon became very sick. Their neighbours were suffering similar difficulties and could only give a little help. But as Jennie's health deteriorated they managed to club together to raise enough money for Mrs Annas to pay for the twenty mile bus ride to Bacolod City.

In October 1985 Jennie was admitted to the general hospital suffering

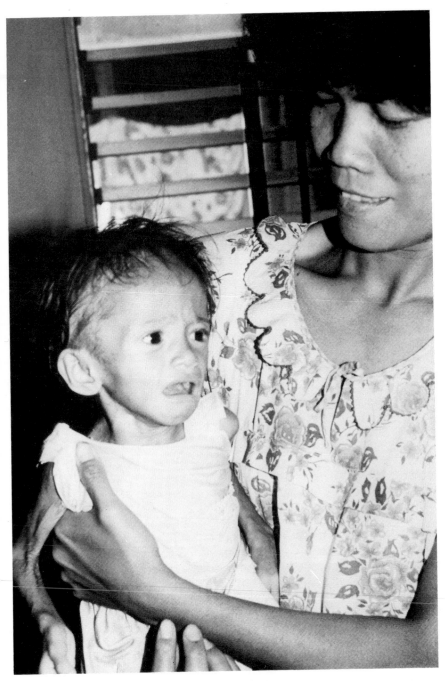

A patient in the malnutrition ward, Bacolod City hospital, Negros.

from severe malnutrition. With careful feeding her condition improved considerably and after six weeks she was considered fit enough to be discharged. She returned home with her mother in the middle of November.

There was just enough work on the **hacienda** to keep some money coming into the family budget but once again the milling season was cut short. Mr Annas found himself without employment early the following year. With a desperate shortage of food in the family Jennie began to lose weight and very soon she had to be re-admitted to hospital.

In May 1986 the malnutrition ward of Bacolod City Hospital was full. Like Jennie Annas most of the children were from families that depend on the sugar industry for their livelihood.

Hunger and misery are not new to the sugar workers of Negros. A survey conducted by the National Secretariat of Social Action in 1984, before the crisis in the industry led to such widespread unemployment, found that 66% of children under seven were malnourished.[1] Most of them were suffering from first (mild) or second (moderate) degree malnutrition. Fears that an increasing number of children would become severely malnourished, as unemployment rose, were well founded. A UNICEF survey in August 1985 found 40% of children under the age of 14 to be severely malnourished.[2] With no resurgence in sugar prices the situation has steadily deteriorated. One year later it was estimated that in some parts of the island as many as 73% of children were malnourished.[3]

Negros used to be one of the richest islands in the Philippines. Its fertile lands and cheap labour provided the base on which a fortunate few grew wealthy by turning the best lands into sugar plantations. But with little left for the production of food or other crops it has always been highly vulnerable to

Feeding programme, Negros.

36

For picking thatch out of harvested cane children can earn 40p a day, often the only source of income for a family.

the type of tragedy that it currently faces.

In 1985 Oxfam joined the international relief operation to supply food, work animals, tools, seeds and fertiliser to the unemployed sugar workers.[4] Feeding centres have been set up in many areas. The target of this supplementary feeding programme is to provide one meal a day to the estimated 85,000 children under six suffering from moderate or severe malnutrition. At the same time every effort is being made to increase food production on the island.[5]

Blame for the current crisis in the Philippines sugar industry can be laid at several different doors. Sugar production and its marketing in the Philippines were the overall responsibility of the corrupt government institutions of the Marcos era. Funds were mis-managed to an extent that would have made it difficult for the industry to survive even under the most favourable market conditions. In addition a national economic crisis caused high rates of inflation. Prices of oil, machinery, spare parts and fertilisers soared and greatly increased the costs of production. But it is the industry's dependence on the US market for trade, a dependence which was first established during the colonial era, that tipped the balance and turned it into a full-scale human tragedy.

THE CANE TRADE

The pattern of trade which was established during colonial days forms the basis for existing trading arrangements. Primary production takes place in former colonies, such as the Philippines, Jamaica and Mauritius, and refining and consumption in Europe and the USA.

About 70% of the world's sugar is consumed in the country where it is produced. The rest is traded either under controlled market agreements or on the world market.

THE MARKET DESTINATION OF SUGAR:

TOTAL PRODUCTION
—APPROXIMATELY 100 MILLION TONNES PER ANNUM OF THIS: APPROXIMATELY 30 MT IS TRADED EACH YEAR. OF THIS:

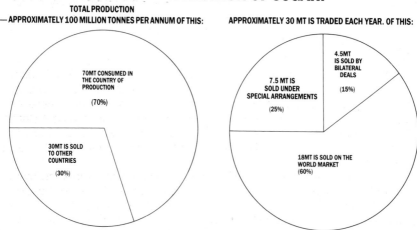

70MT CONSUMED IN THE COUNTRY OF PRODUCTION (70%)

30MT IS SOLD TO OTHER COUNTRIES (30%)

4.5MT IS SOLD BY BILATERAL DEALS (15%)

7.5 MT IS SOLD UNDER SPECIAL ARRANGEMENTS (25%)

18MT IS SOLD ON THE WORLD MARKET (60%)

Source: Sugar Yearbook 1984 Peter Ross 'Sugar Sweet and Sour' Publ. ACOA 1986.

Controlled Market Agreements

There are two types of controlled market agreement; bilateral agreements and special arrangements.

Bilateral Agreements

Most countries, whether exporting or importing sugar, prefer to have a guaranteed market or supply to protect themselves from price fluctuations. They do this by entering into trade agreements with other countries. These agreements generally arrange for an agreed quantity of sugar, at an agreed price, to be imported, or exported, for an agreed period of time. Brazil, for example, had an arrangement with the USSR to deliver 320,000 tonnes of sugar each year between 1981 and 1985.[6]

Special Arrangements

Some countries trade sugar through Special Arrangements, which are essentially multi-lateral agreements. The three most important of these are the Sugar Protocol of the Lomé Convention, the quota system of the USA, and Cuba's trade with the Eastern bloc.

Sugar Protocol of the Lomé Convention

The Lomé Convention was first signed in February 1975 between the European Community (EC) and 64 African, Caribbean and Pacific (ACP) countries. Most of these countries were already linked to the various EC member states through previous trade agreements. Nearly half were Commonwealth countries who signed the Lomé Convention as a way of compensating for trade preferences which they lost when Britain joined the EC.

The Convention includes a wide range of provisions on aid and trade cooperation for promoting the development of the ACP countries. Its trade provision was designed to give ACP exports – which are mostly primary products and raw materials such as oil, copper, iron ore, coffee, sugar, tea, cocoa, groundnuts, cotton and wood – unrestricted access to the Community market.[7]

The Sugar Protocol of the Lomé Convention was implemented to protect those ACP countries that had traditionally exported sugar to Britain under the Commonwealth Sugar Agreement (CSA). The CSA, which was first established in 1951, was the most formal of a long series of preferences granted by Britain to sugar imports from its colonies. Under the CSA Britain undertook to purchase 1.7 million tonnes of sugar each year on a negotiated price quota basis from Australia, the British West Indies, Fiji, Mauritius and South Africa.[8]

When Britain joined the EC the CSA was terminated and replaced by the 1975 Sugar Protocol of the Lomé Convention. This is similar to the Commonwealth Sugar Agreement in that a number of ACP producer countries agree to provide the Community with a specific quantity of sugar each year, which the Community agrees to purchase from them at a guaranteed price.

TATE AND LYLE

Tate and Lyle is Europe's major cane sugar importer. Nearly all the preferential sugar coming into the European Community under the Sugar Protocol is delivered to Tate and Lyle in Britain for refining and marketing with a small quantity (about 12%) going to French refineries.

In 1921 Tate and Lyle formed as a company from a merger between the two principal British refinery enterprises, Henry Tate and Abram Lyle. Their merger meant that they represented 60% of British sugar refining capacity.

In 1936 Tate and Lyle moved into buying plantations on the sugar producing islands of the Caribbean – principally Trinidad and Jamaica. It also built factories, set up technical back up, engineering services, sugar refining machinery and, in 1940, began to transport sugar in bulk from the Caribbean to its refineries in Britain. In 1965 it purchased United Molasses, the largest molasses enterprise in the world. With such a wide range of interests covering the shipping, storage, processing, refining and distribution of sugar, Tate and Lyle is a truly vertically integrated company representing a vital link between Third World producers and European consumers.[1]

In recent years investment climates and trends have changed. In many developing countries foreign ownership of agri-business concerns has become more economically risky (due to unstable world market prices) and politically unacceptable. So Tate and Lyle has abandoned its landholdings and moved into the field of management and consultancy. Through Tate and Lyle Technical Services it manages sugar estates in Zambia, Swaziland, Belize and Jamaica.[2]

When Britain joined the European Community in 1973 Tate and Lyle and others involved in the cane business faced growing competition from the Community's beet producers. The company was vocal in negotiations over the Sugar Protocol which helped secure a continued market for cane sugar. However, imports were reduced from 1.7 million tonnes to 1.3 million tonnes which meant that there was an increased excess of refining capacity for cane sugar in Britain.

Tate and Lyle responded by rationalising the industry. First, it bought up Manbre Garton, the only other significant UK sugar refiner and a major starch producer. Subsequently, in 1980, it was closed down with a loss of 5,000 jobs. Next to go was Tate and Lyle's own Liverpool refinery, with further job losses of 2,000.[3] Tate and Lyle now run two refineries, one at Silvertown in London and one at Greenock in Scotland, with a combined refining capacity of 1.15 million tonnes of raw sugar, employing a workforce of 2,300.

Following the closure of the Liverpool refinery in 1981 the UK no longer had sufficient refining capacity to take all the ACP quota sugar. Tate and Lyle therefore arranged to sell 150,000 tonnes annually to the French refiners and consequently the destination of ACP sugar is split between the French and British refineries. This has helped the future of the ACP arrangements as it has meant that two countries, rather than one, have an interest in cane's survival on the European market.[4]

By pruning down sugar refining and building up other areas such as trading, plastics and liquid bulk storage, Tate and Lyle were able to make an overall pre-tax profit of £81.5 million in 1986, up from £76.7 million the previous year. However, due to the EC's sugar pricing policies their pre-tax profits from sugar refining in the UK have slumped from £19 million in 1983 to only £4.1 million in 1986.[5]

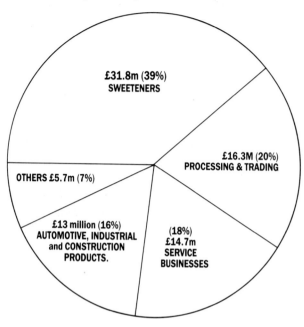

SECTOR Analysis of Tate and Lyle's pre-tax profits in 1986

£31.8m (39%)
SWEETENERS

£16.3M (20%)
PROCESSING & TRADING

OTHERS £5.7m (7%)

£13 million (16%)
AUTOMOTIVE, INDUSTRIAL
and CONSTRUCTION
PRODUCTS.

(18%)
£14.7m
SERVICE
BUSINESSES

Source: Tate and Lyle Annual Report and Accounts

Sweeteners – Tate and Lyle has cane sugar refineries in the UK, Canada, USA, Zimbabwe and Portugal; beet sugar factories in the USA; and plants for the manufacture of cereal sweeteners and starches in Europe.

Processing and Trading – Includes international sugar trading, storage and distribution, the production of speciality animal feeds and malting.

Service Businesses – The packing and distribution of sugar, tea and other products, agribusiness, bulk liquid storage and insurance.

Automotive, Industrial and Construction Products – Automotive parts, plastic and aluminium products for the construction and other industries, custom gears and precision machined components. This is the company's major area of diversification away from sweeteners.

It is an open-ended agreement although there is a provision which allows for the Protocol to be renounced by the Community and/or the ACP countries, providing two years notice is given.[9]

At the time that the Protocol was being negotiated the world price of sugar was considerably higher than the price being offered by the Community. Several ACP countries opted for lower Community quotas than they had enjoyed under the Commonwealth Sugar Agreement. Because of their high cost industries and falling levels of production they needed to take advantage of the then high prices on the world market.

It was finally agreed that the EC would import 1.3 million tonnes of cane sugar of which African producers would provide 51%, Caribbean producers 35% and Pacific producers 13%. The remainder was allocated to India, Belize and St Kitts-Nevis-Anguilla who were signatories to the CSA, but not to Lomé.[10] Since then there have been some minor alterations in the quota allocations between countries.[11]

The size of the Protocol came under discussion when Portugal joined the EC in 1986. Portugal does not have a domestic sugar industry so it imports 200,000 tonnes of raw cane sugar, which, in recent years, have come mainly from Swaziland, Zimbabwe and the Ivory Coast, which it then refines. The Portuguese wanted to maintain these imports to keep their own refining industry alive so they argued for a corresponding increase in the amount of ACP sugar allowed into the European Community.

The EC's Council of Ministers saw differently. They wanted Portugal to take some of the surplus beet sugar that is produced in Europe. It was finally agreed that an additional 75,000 tonnes of ACP sugar, from Swaziland, Zimbabwe, Malawi and the Ivory Coast, would be allowed into Portugal for the seven year transition period, but a permanent increase was refused.[12]

Under the Sugar Protocol ACP countries receive guaranteed prices. These are the same as the prices paid to European beet sugar producers although the ACP producers have to cover the additional freight and insurance costs of transporting the sugar to Europe.

The Protocol also stipulates that any country unable to meet its supply commitments for reasons other than **force majeure** will have its guaranteed allocation reduced by the amount which it is unable to supply. If, however, the ACP producers are able to prove that their inability to deliver is due to factors beyond their control, the Commission can allow an additional period for delivery.[13]

The USA Quota System

The United States has ensured its supplies of sugar by protecting and encouraging its own sugar industry and giving preference to imports from several suppliers of cane sugar, particularly in the Caribbean, Central and South America, and the Philippines. In effect this has meant that most of these countries have developed their sugar industries on the basis that their production could always be sold to the United States. As the US has developed and expanded its own sugar industry, and encouraged the production of maize-based sweeteners, there has been a dramatic drop in imports and these countries have had to seek out other markets.

Historically Cuba and the Philippines have been favoured suppliers of cane sugar to the United States market. In 1902, for example, preference was extended to these two countries through the Reciprocity Treaty. Both expanded their respective industries which increased their dependence on sugar as a source of foreign exchange.

The quota system was established in 1934 by the Jones-Costigan Act. It was an attempt by the United States to organise its supplies of sugar and protect its own growers. An assessment was made each year of the quantity of sugar required, together with a calculation of the price which should be paid. Quotas were then calculated for each sugar producer, whether domestic or foreign, which supplied sugar to the US market. This remained in force until 1948 when the Sugar Act was implemented, based on a commitment to achieve self-sufficiency, stability in supplies and protection to domestic refiners.[14]

In 1974 the Sugar Act was allowed to lapse since world sugar prices were relatively high. As world prices declined in 1977 and 1978, price support measures and import fees were introduced to protect local producers. The quota system was re-introduced in 1982, relating to average shipments to the USA between 1975 and 1981. The overall size of the quota has been dramatically reduced because of increased domestic production and the introduction of High Fructose Corn Syrup.[16]

Cuba's Trade with the Eastern Bloc

Until the 1959 revolution Cuba relied largely on the USA for its exports. It is one of the world's biggest sugar producers and depends almost entirely on sugar for its foreign exchange earnings. After 1959 Cuba set about nationalising its sugar industry and expropriating both foreign and national companies. The US decided to cease all trade with Cuba so the Government began negotiations with the USSR and Eastern bloc countries for an increase in sales.

Under the Agreement that was reached Cuba was granted an assured market for its sugar, at prices adjusted not to the world market, but to the cost of production. Cuba is also permitted to vary its delivery totals so that sugar can be diverted to the free market when world prices are high. It also barters some of its sugar for machinery with the Eastern bloc countries.[16]

The World Market

About 60% (18 million tonnes a year) of exported sugar is not covered by bilateral agreements or special arrangements and is traded on the world market. The amount of sugar traded on the world market increased considerably between 1970 and 1980. Developing country cane producers increased their world market exports from 4.3 million tonnes to about 8 million tonnes. Developed country producers, mostly in the EC, increased their world market exports from 2.6 million tonnes to 6.2 million tonnes.[17]

The reason most sugar producers prefer to trade through bilateral agreements or special arrangements is that it gives them an assured market for their produce, generally at a guaranteed price. Trading on the world market offers no such security.

Depending on levels of supply and demand, prices can fluctuate considerably. Attempts to control world market prices have been made through a succession of International Sugar Agreements (ISAs). However, the present ISA has no provision for controlling prices. The last Agreement which did contain a provision of this kind ran from 1977 to 1984 and attempted to keep them within a range of 13 to 23 US cents per pound.[18]

World market sugar prices have generally followed a six year cycle with peaks in 1951, 1957, 1963, 1974 and 1980. The peaks occur when the demand for sugar rises. The high sugar prices which result encourage increased production, which brings more sugar onto the world market and in turn leads to a fall in prices.

25 YEARS OF WORLD SUGAR PRICES

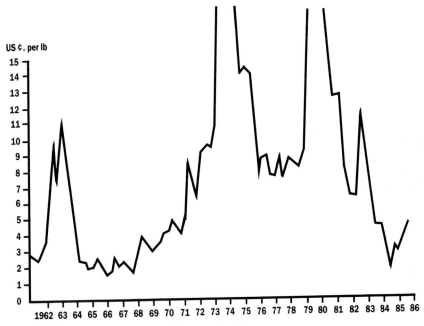

US ¢. per lb

Source: SUGAR REVIEW No. 1736 28 March 1985   C. Czarnikow Ltd.

Since the last peak of 1980 prices have remained very low and show little sign of rising. Because of production increases by the EC and many developing countries, a slowing in consumption growth and an increased use of alternative sweeteners, there is said to be some 40 million tonnes of sugar presently held in stocks. It will take many years before sugar becomes scarce and prices rise.

New Risks for the Producer

As demonstrated by the problems that the Philippines sugar industry faces, this trading structure is full of risks for the developing country cane producers. The protection offered through bilateral agreements or special arrangements is not usually open-ended. There is always the danger that the agreement may be terminated, in the way that the US quota system has been dismantled. To find a buyer the producer then has to turn to the world market, where prices are generally unstable and currently very low.

The days of the colonial era set the patterns of trade for the sugar producing countries, forcing them into a relationship with the colonial powers that was inherently unequal. Post-colonialism maintained that dependency and inequality. But in the second half of the 20th century a new element was introduced into this relationship. The developed world began to intensify its own agricultural production.

In Europe in the late 1960s the European Community established the Common Agricultural Policy (CAP) as the principle mechanism designed to provide support to farmers, improve productivity and increase food supplies. In the United States similar measures were being taken to protect farmers and increase food supplies by price support and tighter controls on imports.

These policies have had a far-reaching effect on the world sugar trade. The EC has so over-stimulated the production of sugar beet that it has swamped the world market with its surpluses. The USA has been so successful in converting its massive maize supplies to liquid sweeteners that it barely needs to import cane sugar any more.

At the same time a pressing need for foreign exchange has led to an increase in cane sugar production in a number of developing countries. The major cane producers, such as Cuba, Thailand, Brazil and India, have been increasing their exports, while traditional importers, such as Sri Lanka, have been endeavouring to become self-sufficient in sugar.

The net effect of these developments is that world prices have tumbled, markets have contracted and the weaker developing country cane producers have suffered tremendous losses.

SUGAR BEET

Nearly 85%, of the world's sugar beet is grown in Europe where the European Community is the largest producer. It accounts for 43% and the USSR for 27% of Europe's total beet supply. The rest of the world's sugar beet comes mostly from North America, and the temperate belt Asian countries such as Afghanistan, China, Iran and Iraq. Some beet is grown in North Africa and a very small amount comes from the southern parts of South America such as Chile and Uruguay.[1]

Beet, as a source of sucrose (sugar) does not have such a long or colourful history as cane. In its natural state it was first found growing along the shores of the Mediterranean in Roman times. But the richness of sugar in beet was not recorded until the 16th century, and it was another 300 years before attempts to refine it commercially were sucessful.

Britain's blockade of the French ports during the Napoleonic wars apparently provided the impetus for the necessary technological advance. Cut off from its colonies, France was suffering from severe sugar shortages. Accordingly, in 1811, Napoleon ordered large areas to be sown with sugar beet and set scientists to work on the problem of refining on a commercial basis.

The French chemist, Benjamin Delessert, was the first to come up with the answer. News of his success sent Napoleon straight to the village of Passay, on January 2nd 1812, to visit Delessert's factory where, in a fit of enthusiasm, he took off his own Legion of Honour to decorate the chemist – or so the story goes. The newspaper *Moniteur Universal* reported that, "A great revolution in the economy of France has started today!".[2] In fact it was a step that changed the face of the world's sugar industry. By 1880 sugar beet had displaced cane as the principal source of sugar in Europe and the growing of sugar beet had spread to other temperate zones including the USA, USSR and Canada.

The British beet industry

There was no similar incentive to develop a beet industry in Britain. Cane sugar supplies from its colonies were plentiful throughout the 18th and 19th centuries although tales of the harsh conditions under which it was being produced caused severe moral indignation among some and caused a group of Quakers to open a sugar beet factory in Essex in 1832 because they disapproved of the slave trade. It was a commercial failure.

It was the sinking of several sugar cargo ships during the First World War and the subsequent sugar shortages that finally gave rise to a British sugar beet industry. A sugar factory was opened in 1920 but 1925 marked the start of the expansion of the industry when the Government introduced a subsidy for beet growers. By 1928 there were factories operating all over South East England, owned and managed by 15 different companies. In 1936 these were merged into one company, British Sugar, which was acquired by S & W Berisford in 1982.

British Sugar owns thirteen beet sugar factories, which are concentrated in two major areas – the East of England and the Midlands. The factories are supplied with beet by about 12,000 farmers. British Sugar employs over 5,000 full-time staff and takes on an additional 2,000 workers during the four month processing season, from November to February.

Before Britain joined the EC in 1973 domestic sugar beet production was restricted to one third of domestic requirements as a way of keeping the market open for the cane producing former colonies. After the expiry of the Commonwealth Sugar Agreement in 1974 and its replacement by the Sugar Protocol of the Lomé Convention, beet production became subject to the rules and regulations of the Common Agricultural Policy's sugar regime. This meant a shift in balance in favour of beet with the result that half of the 2.2 million tonnes of sugar consumed in Britain each year is from beet, and the rest from cane imports.

Chapter 4

Sweet Excess

Sugar beet production
in the European Community

'But however much the EEC huffs and puffs there is little doubt that the enlargement of beet growing in the Community has disrupted the world sugar market and caused considerable economic distress to many developing countries.'

John Edwards, Commodities Editor, Financial Times, 17 August 1982

Chapter 4

SWEET SUCCESS

JIM MILTON is one of the 12,000 farmers in Britain who grow sugar beet. He owns 350 acres of land in Lincolnshire, a prime beet growing area because its rich alluvial soil. He also grows cereals, potatoes, onions, peas, daffodils and soft fruit.

He comes from a farming family and married into a farming family. The farm he owns now is run as a family business. His wife takes care of much of the accounting and day to day management whilst his son, who will take over the business from them, works full time on the farm. They employ five permanent workers and take on extra labour during the spring, when it is most needed.

The Miltons run an efficient, profitable farming business thanks not only to their own efforts but also to Britain's continuing commitment to agricultural support which, since it joined the EC, has been governed by the mechanisms of the Common Agricultural Policy (CAP). The CAP rules that govern sugar production are mainly about supporting farmers and ensuring that they get a good price for their sugar beet which cannot be undercut by cheap imports. This way the CAP aims to maintain a steady flow of EC produced sugar onto the domestic market.

The European Community's leading sugar producer is France which accounts for almost 30% of total production. Sugar beet grows particularly well in the Picardy area of Northern France. The next largest producers are Germany and Italy, with Britain taking fourth place. France and Spain are the only two European sugar cane producers. Spain produces about 10,000 tonnes annually. Cane is also grown in the 'Departments d'Outre-Mer' (The DOM) of Reunion and Guadaloupe, which are constitutionally an integral part of France. Traditionally France had subsidised production in both.[1]

The EC's Sugar Regime operates through a combination of **production quotas** and **price support mechanisms**.

Production Quotas

Every five years the EC's Council of Ministers reviews the level of its production quotas. The quotas are split into '**A' Quota**, which is equal to the level of Community consumption (without taking into account its annual cane sugar imports from the ACP states under the Sugar Protocol of the

Lomé Convention and via Portugal) and **Specialisation** or 'B' Quota which is an additional amount to cover unexpected shortfalls in production or increases in consumption. Together, 'A' and 'B' quota sugar is known as the **maximum quota**. Sugar that is produced in excess of the maximum quota is known as '**C**' **sugar** and has to be exported.

The Council divide the maximum quotas between national governments, who allocate them to processors who, in turn, contract the farmers to supply them with the necessary amounts of beet.

HOW THE EC SUGAR QUOTAS ARE ALLOCATED

QUOTA PERIOD — 1986/87 — 1991/92
(To be reviewed in 1988)

1,000 tonnes WSE (white sugar equivalent)

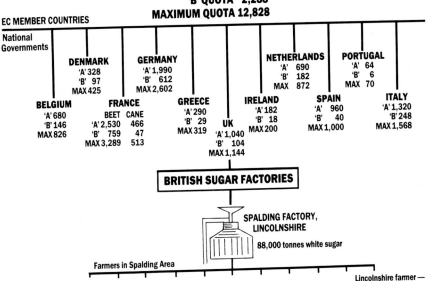

EC COUNCIL OF MINISTERS
'A' QUOTA 10,540
'B' QUOTA 2,288
MAXIMUM QUOTA 12,828

EC MEMBER COUNTRIES

National Governments

DENMARK
'A' 328
'B' 97
MAX 425

GERMANY
'A' 1,990
'B' 612
MAX 2,602

NETHERLANDS
'A' 690
'B' 182
MAX 872

PORTUGAL
'A' 64
'B' 6
MAX 70

BELGIUM
'A' 680
'B' 146
MAX 826

FRANCE
BEET CANE
'A' 2,530 466
'B' 759 47
MAX 3,289 513

GREECE
'A' 290
'B' 29
MAX 319

IRELAND
'A' 182
'B' 18
MAX 200

SPAIN
'A' 960
'B' 40
MAX 1,000

ITALY
'A' 1,320
'B' 248
MAX 1,568

UK
'A' 1,040
'B' 104
MAX 1,144

BRITISH SUGAR FACTORIES

SPALDING FACTORY, LINCOLNSHIRE

88,000 tonnes white sugar

Farmers in Spalding Area

Lincolnshire farmer — 925 tonnes sugar beet

Statistical source: Harris, Simon 'Review of the EC sugar market' Report to World Bank, December 1985 — Annex Table 4.

Price Support Mechanism

Both 'A' and 'B' quota sugar are eligible for Community price support whilst 'C' sugar does not receive Community support.

The support prices are set annually as part of a series of price fixing negotiations for CAP products, which normally finish in April or early May.

Basically two prices have to be worked out. First, the amount to be paid to the farmer for the sugar beet that is delivered to the factory, and second, the amount to be paid to the processor for the white sugar that comes out of the factory ready for sale to the consumer or manufacturer. The latter is calculated from the price that has to be paid to the farmer – as it is the processor who has to pay the farmer – but takes into account the processor's manufacturing margin.

To ensure that producers contribute towards the cost of disposing of surplus sugar, they are charged a producer levy which is split 60:40 between growers and processors. The producer levy on 'A' quota sugar is charged at a low rate of 2% of the intervention price because this sugar is meant to be equivalent to domestic consumption and should not, therefore, need to be exported. The much higher rate of 39.5% is charged on 'B' quota sugar because this is designedly in surplus. Additionally, from 1986/87 an extra **Elimination Levy** is being charged at 1.3% on all quota sugar.

For sugar beet the EC sets, as the initial institutional support price, the basic beet price. This is the amount the processors have to pay the farmers when world prices are high in relation to domestic prices, and producer levies are not necessary. However, as producer levies are nearly always necessary, the EC sets a minimum beet price, which is the basic beet price minus the producer levies.

The cane sugar that comes into the EC fits into the same institutional support system as beet. The ACP countries get paid the raw or white sugar intervention prices. They are exempt from producer levies but have to meet the costs of freight and insurance to get their produce to the EC.

The Miltons have a contract with their local British Sugar factory to deliver

British Sugar factory Lincolnshire.

925 tonnes of sugar beet each year. As Britain has such a small 'B' quota allocation (only 10% of 'A') British Sugar buy sugar beet from the farmers at a flat rate calculated as an average of the two prices.[2] In 1985 the Miltons were paid £26.70 for each tonne of sugar that they delivered to the British Sugar factory which meant that they received £24,697.50 for sugar beet that year, which they estimate to be 20% of their gross income.

To ensure that they will be able to supply the factory with their obligatory 925 tonnes of sugar beet a year the Miltons plant out 50 acres of beet. From this they would normally expect a yield of approximately 1,000 tonnes giving them a surplus of 75 tonnes.

If the factory is short of beet for maximum quota sugar they may buy some, or all, of this at the agreed British contract price of £26.70. More often it is processed into 'C' sugar which is then sold onto the world market. In 1985 farmers received between £6 and £8 a tonne for 'C' sugar, considerably less than the amount they were paid for quota sugar, but it still would have contributed about £500 to the Miltons' income.

SWEET EXCESS

The sugar regime has been successful in protecting the income of EC farmers and ensuring a steady flow of home produced beet onto the domestic market. The EC pays its farmers more than five times the current world market price (5 US cents per pound in October 1986) to grow each pound of sugar. With such high rewards Community farmers have increased annual production from 10.8 million tonnes (raw sugar equivalent) in 1976, when the EC first began to export more sugar than it imported, to 13.8 million tonnes in 1985. In the last eight years it has sold 39 million tonnes of sugar on the world market. Its share of the world market increased massively from 5% in 1972 to 25% in 1985.[3]

EC-10: Sugar Production & Consumption

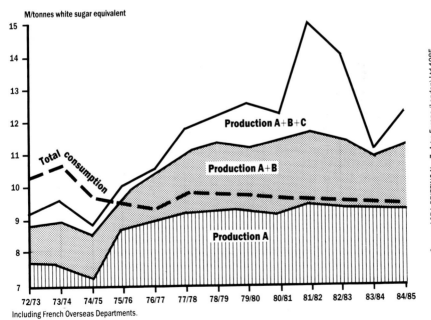

Source: AGRA-BRIEFING No. 7, Agra Europe (London) Ltd 1985

Including French Overseas Departments.

EC PRICING POLICY

In practice it works like this ...

In 1985/86 the EC set the basic beet price at £25.30 for each tonne of sugar beet delivered to the factory. When farmers deliver their consignment of 'A' quota beet they are paid £25.30, less the producer levy of 2% (51p), which makes £24.79. This represents the minimum beet price per tonne paid for 'A' quota sugar. When they deliver 'B' quota sugar to the factory the payment is £25.30 minus 39.5% producer levy (£9.99) which makes £15.30 – the minimum beet price paid for 'B' quota sugar. No price support will be given for 'C' sugar which will be sold at world market prices.

The EC pays for the processed beet – the white sugar – that leaves the factory, so that the processors can pay the farmers the minimum beet price. It works out how much to pay for this sugar by a complex series of calculations.

The starting point is the basic beet price. On to this is added the costs of transport, reception at the factory and processing, to arrive at the intervention price. This is the level at which the national intervention agencies have an open-ended obligation to buy all EC quota sugar offered to them. It varies slightly from area to area to take into account the cost of transporting the sugar from surplus to deficit areas (i.e. Italy, UK, Ireland and Portugal).

The intervention price forms the floor to domestic market prices for white sugar. It serves as the base for setting the threshold price for white sugar, which is 7% higher, and acts as the ceiling to domestic market prices. These two form the outer limits of the support price band within which internal EC market prices fluctuate.

But the EC also needs to ensure that sugar flows onto the market smoothly all the year round despite the fact that beet is only being produced during approximately three months of the year. To do this there is a storage cost levy/reimbursement scheme. Processors are charged a storage cost tax. This money is then used to pay a monthly storage refund on all stocks of sugar, which ensures that processors and traders find it worthwhile to store sugar and release it slowly onto the market.

White sugar is finally marketed in the Community at an effective support price, which is the intervention price plus the storage cost levy.

Incorporated into the regime are other mechanisms designed to ensure that both producers and consumers are insulated from the world market. To guard against cheap imports which could undercut domestic market prices the EC sets a threshold price. This is substantially higher than the target price and represents the minimum price at which sugar can be imported into the Community. It is enforced by a variable import levy – a tax on imports that represents the difference between the world price and the threshold price.

The variable export levy works in reverse. It comes into operation when world market prices are higher than domestic prices. It is a tax on the gain EC producers would make if they sold their sugar on the world market rather than within the Community. As such it is designed to protect the consumer from rising prices.

Sources: Harris, Simon (1983), **The EC Sugar Regime**, Report for the FAO, Rome.
Harris, Simon (1985), **Review of the EC Sugar Market**, Report for the World Bank.

How the surplus has built up

The surplus began to build up during the second production quota period which ran from 1975/76 to 1980/81. It was set for a Community of nine, rather than six, as Britain, Ireland and Denmark had all joined the EC in 1973. As it was being negotiated in 1974/75 there was a world sugar shortage. World market prices rose well above those being paid for sugar in the Community, and the Council of Ministers over-reacted by making every effort to ensure increased production. They raised quotas, reduced producer levies and increased support prices.

At the same time improvements at farm and factory level were leading to higher sugar yields. New, higher-yielding seed varieties, better husbandry techniques, improved machinery and increased use of pesticides meant that sugar beet yields – in tonnes of beet per hectare – were increasing. (see Table) At factory level processing was becoming more efficient as new factories were built and old ones modernised:

	Sugar beet yields tonnes per/ha	White sugar yields tonnes per/ha
1968/69-1970/71	42.98	5.65
1982/83-1984/85	50.16	6.97

Source: Harris, Simon (1985), Review of the EC Sugar Market, Report to the World Bank, page 33

The net result was that production in the Community rose from 9 million tonnes in 1974 to 13.5 million tonnes by the end of the second quota period in 1980. During the same period there was also an abrupt halt in the growth of EC sugar consumption. The peak of 11.6 million tonnes recorded in 1974 fell back to a level of about 10.5 million tonnes, where it has remained. The consequence of these developments was that Community self-sufficiency in sugar had risen to 130% by 1980/81.

Attempts to cut production during the third quota period, (which was being negotiated for a Community of ten since Greece's accession in 1981) were wholly unsuccessful. Member countries did not want to relinquish their profitable 'A' quotas, which were, in fact, slightly increased. 'B' quotas were slightly reduced, with Britain taking the largest cut.

Community production rose sharply in 1981, to 15.4 million tonnes. This meant that the Community had produced 5 million tonnes more than it needed. It remained the same in 1982 then production fell to around 12 million tonnes in 1983 but had risen to 13.8 million tonnes in 1985.[4]

Negotiations for the fourth quota period (1986/87 to 1990/91) took place in the latter half of 1985 against a gloomy background of huge sugar surpluses – forcing down world market prices – and mounting costs to the Community for export subsidies. Taking into account its ACP cane imports of 1.3 million tonnes a year the EC was producing 4.3 million tonnes of surplus sugar each year. World stocks of sugar were at an all time high of some 50 million tonnes. The producer levies on 'A' and 'B' sugar were failing to meet the full cost of exporting all these surpluses and a deficit of £228 million (Ecu 400 million) had accumulated over the past five years.[5]

It was agreed that the producer levy deficit should be paid off by those countries which had contributed to it, i.e. those which had produced the most surplus, or 'C', sugar over the period in which it was accumulated. This was the Elimination Levy, charged at a rate of 1.3% on all quota sugar. As far as the quotas were concerned it was argued that as Community production had stabilised there was no need to cut them. It was also argued that the accession of Spain and Portugal would soak up some of the surplus and that the chemical industry would be increasing its use of sugar by half a million tonnes over the course of the next five years.

The following table shows which countries have produced most of the surplus: (Insert 'C' sugar table: 'Who produced the surplus')

The Dutch were the only ones to argue for a reduction in quotas as a way of cutting back on surplus production. Britain, Ireland, Greece and Italy all wanted their own quotas to be increased as theirs do not cover consumption. The final decision was to leave the current quota system unchanged for the next two years – 1986/87 to 1988/89 – when it will be reviewed for the last three years of the quota period.[6]

Unlike grain, butter, milk powder or beef, there is no such thing as an EC 'sugar mountain' for the simple reason that surplus production is disposed of by selling it on the world market. The difference between the 20 US cents a pound that the EC farmers are paid for sugar and the five cents or so that it fetches on the world market is met by European producers who lose about £233 for each tonne sold.[7] However, they recover this principally through the high domestic prices charged to consumers.

Whilst European consumers have every right to complain, the real losers are developing country sugar cane producers. In disposing of its surpluses on the world market the European Community has made a major contribution to the slump in world market prices with serious consequences for many Third World producers.

'C' Sugar Production by EC Member Countries from crop year 1968/69 to 1984/85
(1,000 tonnes white sugar equivalent)

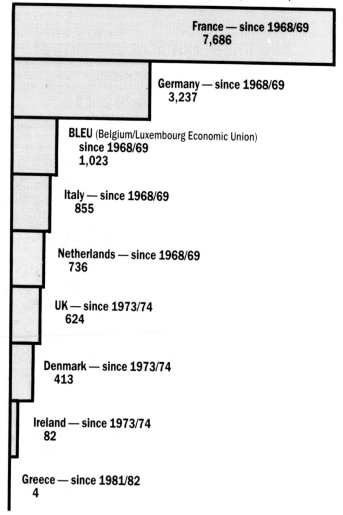

France — since 1968/69
7,686

Germany — since 1968/69
3,237

BLEU (Belgium/Luxembourg Economic Union)
since 1968/69
1,023

Italy — since 1968/69
855

Netherlands — since 1968/69
736

UK — since 1973/74
624

Denmark — since 1973/74
413

Ireland — since 1973/74
82

Greece — since 1981/82
4

Source: Harris, Simon. *Review of the EC Sugar Market*.
Report prepared for the World Bank December 1985

Chapter 5

Bitter Sweet

The impact of EC agricultural policies on developing country sugar producers

'Sugar, then, is the most notable addiction in history that killed not the consumer but the producer.'

Henry Hobhouse *'Seeds of Change'*

Chapter 5

THE EUROPEAN COMMUNITY'S SUGAR REGIME is fundamentally contra-dictory in the way in which it relates to developing country cane producers. On the one hand, it gives preferential trade to a handful of countries under the Sugar Protocol of the Lomé Convention. On the other hand, in failing to exercise restraint over its own production of sugar beet, it has contributed directly to chronically low world market prices for sugar which have led to considerable hardship for many Third World producers. In considering its impact on developing countries it is therefore necessary to distinguish between those countries that do, and those countries that do not have access to the EC market.

THIRD WORLD COUNTRIES WITH ACCESS TO THE EC MARKET

Departments d'Outre Mer (DOM)

Since the sugar regime came into full operation a small amount of **cane** sugar has been included as part of the EC's total sugar supply. This sugar comes from the **Departments d'Outre-Mer** which include Reunion, in the Indian Ocean, and Martinique and Guadeloupe in the Caribbean. As France had traditionally subsidised production in the DOM, their production had to be absorbed into the EC's sugar regime. At first the DOM were producing about 420,000 tonnes a year. Since then production has declined steadily to around 280,000 tonnes (1983/84 to 1985/86 average production).[1] Guadeloupe has developed aubergines as an export crop and Martinique has taken land out of cane and planted bananas and pineapples instead, for which they have a guaranteed market in France.[2]

DOM sugar is refined in France at the two remaining French refineries at Nantes and Marseilles. A third, in Bordeaux, shut down in 1983. With production shrinking the future of these refineries looks uncertain.[3]

The African, Caribbean and Pacific (ACP) countries

Under the Sugar Protocol of the Lomé Convention it was agreed to allow 1.3 million tonnes of raw cane sugar into the Community each year, divided between fifteen ACP countries. The Protocol reflected a stated commitment

on behalf of the EC "to have at heart the interests of those countries whose economies depend to a considerable degree on exports of primary products, notably sugar."[4]

However, the allocation of the 1.3 million tonnes between the ACP countries is very unevenly spread. Negotiations were taking place at a time when world market prices were three times higher than the price being offered by the EC and as a result several countries were happy to opt for lower quotas than they had previously enjoyed.[5] Five countries, Mauritius, Fiji, Guyana, Jamaica and Swaziland, account for 80% of the total quota and Mauritius alone supplies more than one third of the ACP's export allowance to the EC. (See Table)

Several of the ACP countries produce less sugar than they consume so have to import sugar bought on the world market in order to meet their EC quotas. This sets up a bizarre chain reaction whereby the sugar is bought from the world market, sold to the EC and re-exported back onto the world market. The World Bank estimated that in 1981/82 it cost US $42 million to shift sugar around this circle.[6]

The ACP Cane Country preferential import quotas – 1985

	Tonnes white sugar equivalent 1985[1]	Percentage of total quota	Exports not under Special Arrangements as a % of prodtn[2]
Mauritius	90,000	37.5%	3.54%
Fiji	165,000	12.6%	46.16%
Guyana	159,000	12.2%	19.77%
Jamaica	118,000	9.0%	0.00%
Swaziland	117,000	8.9%	48.73%
Barbados	50,000	3.8%	6.47%
Trinidad	44,000	3.4%	0.00%
Belize	40,000	3.1%	32.65%
Zimbabwe	30,000	2.3%	36.95%
Malawi	21,000	1.6%	26.03%
St Kitts	15,000	1.1%	8.28%
Madagascar	11,000	0.9%	0.75%
Tanzania	10,000	0.8%	0.00%
Congo	10,000	0.8%	0.00%
Ivory Coast	10,000	0.8%	34.54%
India[3]	10,000	0.8%	5.54%
Kenya	5,000	0.4%	6.61%
Total	1,305,000	100.0%	

[1] Figures supplied by Tate and Lyle
[2] Simon Harris, Address to OUTLOOK '85, Washington DC, USA, 5th December 1984.
[3] India is not an ACP country but as it was a member of the Commonwealth Sugar Agreement it has been allowed to continue to export to the EC.

Unequally distributed as the benefits are, the Protocol does afford these seventeen countries significant protection from the vagaries of the world market. It is of vital economic importance to Mauritius, for example, which sends 85% of its sugar exports to the EC. It also provides a livelihood for more than a quarter of a million people, which is approximately the number of sugar workers it takes to produce the 1.3 million tonnes of ACP sugar that is exported to the European Community.

Since the period when the Lomé Convention Sugar Protocol was first negotiated world prices have slumped to way below the cost of production in most countries. The Guaranteed Price under the Protocol has, therefore, enabled its beneficiaries to maintain a certain level of export earnings from sugar despite long periods of low world market prices. However, as the table shows, many of these same countries also export to the world market, as a proportion of their exports is not covered by special arrangements.

Since the Protocol was negotiated in 1974 the European Community has shifted from being a net importer of sugar to being the world's largest sugar producer. Given this, the position of ACP sugar in the EC market may be precarious. Over 80% of the Community's raw cane imports are refined, and consumed, in the UK. Although the Sugar Protocol is a Community commitment it could be argued that the future of cane in Europe rests ultimately on the commitment of successive British governments to continue to allow half of the UK's need for sugar to be met through cane imports.

The principal European cane refiner, Tate and Lyle, is a large multinational company with diverse interests. Its future commitment to cane refining will inevitably depend on profitability. The problem for Third World cane producers is that refining provides a diminishing share of Tate and Lyle's profits, accounting for only 5% in 1986.[7] One reason for this is that because of the way in which the EC pricing system works, the profit margin on cane sugar refining is low, roughly a quarter of that on beet sugar processing.

The EC's institutional support price for white sugar is the same for beet and cane sugar. However, Tate and Lyle has to pay the ACP countries a much higher price for its raw cane imports than British Sugar has to pay farmers for the sugar beet that they deliver to the factory. Although it costs much more to process beet than it does to refine cane (because the cane is

Cost of Producing one tonne of sugar 1985

— — — — — —Price Paid by the Consumer £432 — — — — — — —

£362
Gross Operating Margin £60

Profit £11 (3%)

£302
Cost of ACP raw cane imports

£362 Community Support Price

Profits £46 (12.7%)

Gross Operating Margin £144

£218
Cost of beet at factory

TATE & LYLE (cane)   **BRITISH SUGAR (beet)**

1 tonne raw sugar = 920 kilos — white sugar equivalent

63

already partially refined when it is shipped to Europe) this means that there is a much higher gross operating margin on beet, and therefore more opportunity to cut costs. As a result, in 1985 British Sugar made a pre-tax profit of £46 for each tonne of beet sugar it processed, while Tate and Lyle's pre-tax profits were only £11 per tonne.[8]

With this disparity in profit margins British Sugar could theoretically lower its retail price and force Tate and Lyle UK refineries out of business. British Sugar claim that in the event of this happening it would be technically feasible and commercially viable to refine ACP imports in their own factories.[9] However, the danger of this would be a direct conflict of interests, between beet and cane, in which the less profitable cane imports would be at a severe disadvantage.

For ACP sugar exporters, such a high level of dependence on individual company profits and domestic market-share agreements, is undesirable. However, given the realities of the present market structure, their interests are probably best served by the maintenance of Tate and Lyle's UK refining business. Should Tate and Lyle either decide to pull out of the cane refining business, because of diminishing profits, or be forced out by a price war with British Sugar, or should the UK quota allowance change in favour of beet, the future of the ACP sugar exports to the EC could look decidedly uncertain. The livelihood of more than a quarter of a million cane sugar workers in the Third World, in addition to the jobs of several thousand workers in the British cane refining industry would be in jeopardy.

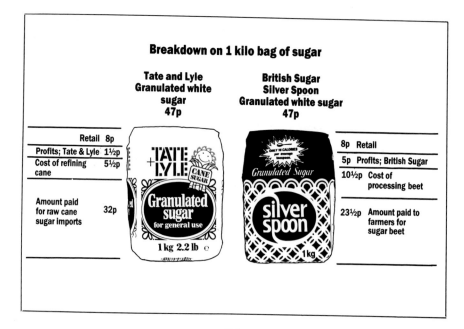

Breakdown on 1 kilo bag of sugar

Tate and Lyle Granulated white sugar 47p

British Sugar Silver Spoon Granulated white sugar 47p

Retail	8p
Profits; Tate & Lyle	1½p
Cost of refining cane	5½p
Amount paid for raw cane sugar imports	32p

8p	Retail
5p	Profits; British Sugar
10½p	Cost of processing beet
23½p	Amount paid to farmers for sugar beet

IMPACT OF THE EC SUGAR REGIME ON COUNTRIES WITHOUT ACCESS TO THE EC MARKET

There is a direct correlation between the rise in European beet production and the fall in world market prices. Although the EC's sugar regime cannot be held entirely responsible for the unprecedented slump in world market prices in 1985, it has been widely acknowledged to have played a key role.[10]

Increased EC production was the main reason for the rise in sugar exports from industrialised countries from 14% of the world total in 1974 to 30% in 1984, thus taking a sizeable share of the market away from developing country exporters.[11]

With prices at less than 3 US cents per pound for part of 1985 even the lowest cost producers could not have been expected to break even. The following table indicates which Third World cane producing countries are most susceptible to a period of sustained low world market prices. The higher the percentage of production which is exported onto the world market without the protection of special arrangements, the higher the risks.

The fall in world sugar prices has meant a loss in export earnings for many producers. The Group of Latin American and Caribbean Sugar Exporting Countries (Gelpacea) reported that their share of world sugar exports fell from 55% in 1974 to 46% in 1983. In 1975 dollar terms, export earnings of member countries fell dramatically from US $6 billion in 1974 to $900 million in 1984.[12]

The loss of export earnings resulting from low sugar prices has increased many countries' problems in repaying their international debts. Brazil, for example, produces nearly 10% of the world's sugar. About 30% of its sugar is exported, but only a small proportion of that is protected from the vagaries of the world market by special arrangements. The rest is traded on the world market (see table). It is also one of the world's leading debtor nations. In 1980 4.7% of Brazil's export earnings came from sugar. In 1983 that proportion had fallen to 1.6%.[13]

In 1984 the Philippines cut back its production by nearly half because of low world market prices. This also represented a considerable loss of export earnings as it relies on sugar for between 8% and 10% of these. With 1984/85 production at around 1.6 million tonnes, down from 2.5 million tonnes the previous year, there is a considerably smaller margin for export after domestic consumption has accounted for 1.3 million tonnes. This has serious implications for repayments on an external debt of US $26 billion.[14] But, as already seen, the implications for the people in the Philippines are even more serious.

Indicators of countries' apparent susceptibility to a period of sustained depressed world prices

	Proportion of Production[a] Exported	Proportion of Exports under Special Arrangements[b]	Exports not under Special Arrangements as % of production
Argentina	36.66%	16.65%	30.56%
Barbados	83.62%	92.26%	6.47%
Belize	93.24%	64.98%	32.65%
Bolivia	15.80%	51.07%	7.73%
Brazil	30.34%	12.14%	26.66%
Colombia	19.97%	21.46%	15.69%
Congo	63.90%	143.38%	0.00%
Costa Rica	29.35%	82.14%	5.24%
Cuba	92.20%	74.38%	23.62%
Dominican Republic	74.14%	45.56%	40.36%
Ecuador	7.10%	144.69%	0.00%
El Salvador	30.94%	102.60%	0.00%
Fiji	91.51%	49.56%	46.16%
Gabon	14.79%	492.19%	0.00%
Guatemala	50.92%	39.07%	31.03%
Guyana	86.84%	77.23%	19.77%
Haiti	13.59%	172.63%	0.00%
Honduras	44.61%	48.74%	22.87%
India	5.91%	6.31%	5.54%
Ivory Coast	42.69%	19.07%	34.54%
Jamaica	69.86%	109.38%	0.00%
Kenya	7.87%	16.01%	6.61%
Madagascar	22.81%	96.71%	0.75%
Malawi	55.53%	53.12%	26.03%
Mauritius	87.70%	95.96%	3.54%
Mexico	0.37%	109.09%	0.00%
Mozambique	30.98%	76.89%	7.16%
Nicaragua	42.02%	5.48%	39.72%
Pakistan	0.00%	—	0.00%
Panama	56.23%	55.72%	24.90%
Papua New Guinea	18.89%	500.22%	0.00%
Paraguay	7.34%	182.90%	0.00%
Peru	10.24%	176.66%	0.00%
Philippines	49.71%	26.09%	36.74%
St. Kitts-Nevis-Anguilla	92.58%	91.06%	8.28%
Swaziland	90.48%	46.14%	48.73%
Taiwan	39.00%	9.62%	35.25%
Tanzania	9.40%	101.30%	0.00%
Thailand	67.48%	2.10%	66.06%
Trinidad and Tobago	71.86%	151.56%	0.00%
Uganda	0.00%	—	0.00%
Uruguay	4.96%	225.00%	0.00%
Venezuela	0.00%	—	0.00%
Zimbabwe	50.32%	26.58%	36.95%

Note: (a) Average production and exports for the three years 1981 to 1983.
(b) 1984/85 US Import Quotas, the EEC's Lome Convention Quotas and average Cuban Special Arrangement exports for 1981 to 1983.

Source: Simon Harris, (1986) Some Current Issues in the World Sugar Economy
Address to a Conference, 'Crisis and change in the International Sugar Economy'.

ALTERNATIVE SWEETENERS

Sugar is useful for many reasons other than satisfying our sweet tooth. It acts as a preservative in jams, pickles and confectionery because it prevents microbacterial growth. It is readily fermentable by yeasts which makes it important for brewing, breadmaking and baking. It gives crunch to biscuits and bulk to cakes and puddings. It is clear, colourless and odourless, dissolves, dilutes, stores well and is relatively cheap and, of course, provides calories.

But for manufacturers some of these properties are not always desirable. Some want food produced without colour changes. Others wish to provide sweetness without calories. So it was a combination of manufacturer and consumer demands, together with a sugar shortage in 1974 and subsequent price rises, which did most to boost the development of the alternative sweetener market.[1]

In terms of their commercial impact alternative sweeteners fall into two categories; cereal based sweeteners and artificial sweeteners.

Cereal based sweeteners

Cereal based sweeteners are derived traditionally from the wet milling of maize or wheat to produce starch. This in turn is modifed to produce glucose, dextrose (crystallized glucose) and, since the 1970s, high fructose, known in the EC as 'isoglucose'.

In its crude form the chemistry for the conversion of cereals to sweeteners has been known for many years. Starch sweeteners were being produced in the United States before the civil war. As early as 1927 it was recorded that corn syrup and dextrose together accounted for about 11% of sweetener consumption in the US. So even then the starch sweeteners were of competitive significance to beet and cane producers.[2]

Glucose and Dextrose

Glucose is found naturally in many fruits, but especially in grapes. It is also manufactured from maize. It is only half as sweet as sugar but is widely used in the confectionery industry because it promotes chewiness and increases shelf life.

In the EC approximately 1.3 million tonnes of glucose and dextrose are produced each year and this amount has remained constant since the beginning of the 1970s.[3] Similarly, in the USA the production and consumption of these products has remained fairly constant at around 14% of total calorific consumption over the last decade. The market for glucose and dextrose appears to be established and stable.

Isoglucose

The major growth in the alternative sweetener industry has come from the development of isoglucose – known as High Fructose Corn Syrup (HFCS) in the USA – as the result of a technological breakthrough in the 1950s.

Medical researchers testing the metabolism of sugar in the human body discovered that a particular enzyme transformed dextrose into fructose. Fructose is sweeter than either dextrose or sucrose and is more easily assimilated by the body. Ten years later Japanese researchers discovered how to produce this commercially as an alternative to cane and beet sugar. The US company, Standard Brands, bought the patent rights and began production on a small scale in 1967.[4]

A further ten years elapsed before various technological improvements made the production of isoglucose more economical. This was due to two factors. Firstly, legal action taken against Standard Brands in 1975 meant that the basic patent coverage for the conversion of glucose to fructose was removed, which cleared the way for its more general industrial use. Secondly, world sugar shortages in 1974 caused the price of sugar to rise dramatically, at one point peaking at 66 US cents per pound.[5] This gave added incentive to expanding isoglucose production. Several companies in the United States built isoglucose plants in response to this situation but when sugar prices fell in 1975 they found themselves with excess capacity and without a competitive edge over beet and cane.

A breakthrough in 1978 enabled isoglucose producers to increase their market share and put the industry into an expansive phase once again. Until then isoglucose could be produced containing only 42% fructose because that was the point at which the enzyme stops acting on the dextrose. But it was discovered that by a further process it was possible to produce a syrup that was 90% fructose, said to be one and a half times as sweet as sucrose. By blending this 90% syrup with the 42% syrup a product containing 55% fructose was produced. This most recent discovery opened up new industrial uses for isoglucose – such as in the manufacturing of soft drinks – in which it could directly replace sucrose.

It is the development of isoglucose that has posed the most serious threat to cane and beet producers.

Artificial Sweeteners

To simply satisfy a sweet tooth it is not necessary to cut cane, dig beet or harvest maize. Sweetness can also be constructed out of molecules in a laboratory. The main consumer attractions of artificial sweeteners are that they do not contain calories or cause dental caries.

Saccharin

Saccharin was the first artificial sweetener. It was discovered by American chemists in 1879, and was used as a sweetener for about 80 years before it came under attack on health grounds.

Cyclamate

Cyclamate was next to come onto the market. It was used in combination with saccharin but was banned in both the US and Britain by 1970 when it was found to cause cancer of the bladder in mice. Some countries such as Australia and Canada remain unconvinced by the evidence and have since lifted their bans. European manufacturers make and sell over 2,000 tonnes of cyclamate each year but sell none to Britain where the ban remains in force.

Aspartame

Aspartame was discovered by Searle laboratories in the US in 1965. It was approved as a table sweetener in Britain in 1974, but banned a year later on health grounds. The ban was lifted in 1981 and it is now widely sold under the brand name of Nutrasweet. It remains controversial on health grounds and due to its composition its uses are limited to foods with a quick turnover – such as soft drinks and fruit yoghurts – which do not require cooking, as aspartame breaks down at high temperatures.

Acesulfam K

It seemed that at least some of these problems could be overcome with the discovery of acesulfam K (trade name Sunnett) in 1967. Tests so far have not shown any risks to health. It is stable in water, does not decompose when heated and has been approved for use as a general sweetener.

Thaumatin

Thaumatin comes from the African plant **ketemfe**. It is 3,000 times sweeter than sugar and much sweeter than the other artificial sweeteners. It was approved as an artificial sweetener in the UK in 1983 where it has been developed by Tate and Lyle. It is mainly used as a flavour enhancer and in animal foods.[6]

Sucralose

Tate and Lyle have also been developing an artificial sweetener that is derived from sugar. By rearranging the sugar molecule and adding chlorine atoms they have come up with 'Sucralose'. The company expects its product to be approved for sale in Britain soon.[7]

In the European Community artificial sweeteners have not greatly reduced sugar consumption. Their use in diet foods is regulated by some EC member states. In Italy, for example, products containing aspartame and saccharin can only be bought in pharmacies. In many of the other products in which they are being used, such as toothpaste, cosmetics and mouthwashes, they are not actually replacing sugar. Also the sugar industry has successfully played on the image of artificial sweeteners as unnatural products with potential health hazards. They are much more widely used in the USA where the market for diet drinks is firmly established.

Chapter 6

The Real Thing

The growth of the isoglucose industry and its impact on developing country sugar production

'"Are you hungry Sir?"
Hunger? What do we know
about that? Hunger in
villages where fields
are lush with sugar cane!
Hunger which slowly sucks
the life of a people!'
Extract from *A Poem from Negros* by Jean Fallon, Maryknoll Sister, August 1985.

Chapter 6

IN 1985 NEGROS became known as The Ethiopia of South East Asia. The Philippines sugar industry, already facing problems of corruption under the Marcos regime, had been devastated by dramatic cuts in United States' cane imports. A quarter of a million sugar workers found themselves without work and Oxfam joined the relief operation to provide food to an island stricken with hunger and misery.

But the cruel reality for developing countries like the Philippines, which have always depended on the US market for their sugar exports, is that the United States needs to import less and less cane sugar. It is only a matter of time before it will be able to stop importing sugar altogether.

In the last decade it has become technically possible and commercially viable to produce 'sugar' from maize. The product, known in the US as High Fructose Corn Syrup (HFCS) (and as isoglucose in the European Community), has taken a huge share of the US sweetener market away from sugar.

Between 1975 and 1985 HFCS has increased its share of the US market from a negligible 4%, to one third. Sugar's share was decreased from three quarters, to under half.

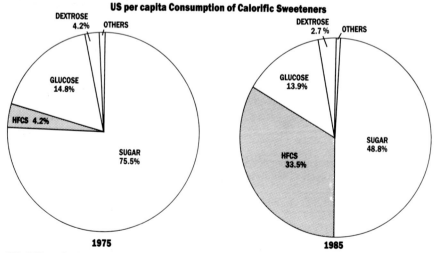

US per capita Consumption of Calorific Sweeteners

DEXTROSE 4.2% OTHERS

GLUCOSE 14.8%

HFCS 4.2%

SUGAR 75.5%

1975

DEXTROSE 2.7% OTHERS

GLUCOSE 13.9%

HFCS 33.5%

SUGAR 48.8%

1985

HFCS — High Fructose Corn Syrup (Isoglucose)

72

The United States produces approximately five and a half million tonnes of sugar a year. The increased use of HFCS caused sugar consumption to fall by nearly three million tonnes between 1975 and 1985. As the following table shows, the US responded by cutting its cane imports.

U.S.A.

| | (Million tonnes raw value) | | |
	Production	Imports	Consumption
1975	5.9	3.5	9.1
1980	5.3	3.8	9.3
1985	5.4	2.2	7.2

(Source: Sugar Year Books 1977 and 1985)

Since 1985 imports have been further reduced, to 1.1 million tonnes in 1987.[1]

For food and drinks manufacturing industries, the main users in the United States, there have been compelling economic reasons for replacing cane imports with domestically produced High Fructose Corn Syrup. The US is the world's largest producer of maize, the raw material used for HFCS. Farm prices for maize fell by nearly 50% between 1981 and 1985, which made HFCS highly competitive with sugar, for which producers are paid support prices of between 18 and 20 US cents a pound.[2]

High Fructose Corn Syrup began to gain significant ground over sugar in 1980 when Coca Cola and Pepsi Cola, the two largest soft drinks companies in the US, announced that they would replace half of the sugar they use in their soft drinks with HFCS. Four years later they switched completely to HFCS.

This was a major blow to beet and cane producers who had always relied on the soft drinks industry to use about 2.4 million tonnes of sugar a year, about one quarter of total US consumption. By 1985 the soft drinks industry accounted for 62% of all sales of HFCS, with the canning and processed foods industries and, to a lesser extent, confectionery, taking their share of the rest.[3]

Until recently it seemed that HFCS had gained its maximum share of the US market. The reason for this was that the technology required to convert the liquid fructose syrup into a dry, granulated form had not been developed. This limited its use to the food and drinks industries and excluded it from the domestic market.

However, scientists in the US have now developed a way of crystallizing HFCS. It is estimated that the product they have come up with so far will take a further half a million tonnes a year of sweetener consumption away from sugar by 1990.[4] It could take an even larger share of the market away from sugar once the technology to granulate fructose has been perfected.

73

The US has made room for HFCS by cutting back on its cane sugar imports. It did this by re-introducing a quota system in 1982 and making annual reductions in individual country's quota allocations.

The quotas were allocated to forty countries, all of which are developing country producers, apart from Australia, South Africa and Canada. However, nine countries account for 80% of all imports and four of these, Australia, the Dominican Republic, the Philippines and Brazil, for 60%.

US Sugar Import Quotas — Quantity and Value

	Oct 82–Sept 83 (12 mths)	Oct 83–Sept 84 (12 mths)	Oct 84–Nov 85 (14 mths)	Dec 85–Dec 86 (13 mths)	Jan 87–Dec 87 (12 mths)
QUOTA ALLOCATION (SHORT TONS)					
Argentina	120400	130806	109220	73788	39130
Australia	232400	252486	210820	142428	75530
Brazil	406000	441090	368300	248820	131950
Dominican Republic	492800	535392	447040	302016	160160
El Salvador	72800	89163	74561	49999.8	26019.8
Guatemala	134400	146016	121190	82368	43680
Panama	81200	88218	73600	49764	26390
Peru	114800	124722	104140	70356	37310
Philippines	378000	410670	342900	231660	143780
Others	859800	956427	825069	598854.2	317480.2
TOTAL	2892600	3174990	2676840	1850054	1001430
World Sugar Price (c/lb, ISA DP)	7.93	6.30	3.99	5.98	7.39
Preferential Price (c/lb)	18.73	19.17	18.27	19.56	19.78
Value of Quota (US$ MN)					
Argentina	26.01	33.67	31.20	20.05	9.70
Australia	50.20	64.99	60.23	38.70	18.72
Brazil	87.70	113.54	105.22	67.60	32.70
Dominican Republic	106.44	137.81	127.71	82.06	39.69
El Salvador	15.72	22.95	21.30	13.58	6.45
Guatemala	29.03	37.58	34.62	22.38	10.82
Panama	17.54	22.71	21.03	13.52	6.54
Peru	24.80	32.10	29.75	19.12	9.25
Philippines	81.65	105.71	97.96	62.94	35.63
Others	185.72	246.18	235.71	162.70	78.67
TOTAL	624.80	817.24	764.73	502.65	248.15
Quota as Percentage of GDP					
Argentina	0.02%	0.02%	0.02%	0.01%	0.00%
Australia	0.03%	0.03%	0.02%	0.01%	0.01%
Brazil	0.03%	0.04%	0.03%	0.02%	0.01%
Dominican Republic	1.23%	1.51%	1.17%	0.73%	0.34%
El Salvador	0.42%	0.58%	0.44%	0.27%	0.13%
Guatemala	0.32%	0.40%	0.36%	0.22%	0.10%
Panama	0.37%	0.47%	0.35%	0.22%	0.10%
Peru	0.13%	0.16%	0.12%	0.07%	0.03%
Philippines	0.18%	0.24%	0.19%	0.12%	0.07%

Source: Sweetener Analysis, January 1987, Landell Mills Commodity Studies.

The quota reductions since 1983/84 are large (from 3.1 million tonnes in 1983/84 to 1 million tonnes in 1987), and all countries have shared in them. Equally impressive, however, is the decline in the value of the quota. In 1983/84 the total sugar quota was worth US$817 million, which represents a considerable transfer of resources from US consumers to the sugar exporting countries. In 1987 the total value was only US$248 million.[5]

As the US has reduced its imports these countries have had to divert their sugar onto the world market. Whilst the US pays between 18 and 20 US cents per pound for raw sugar imports, world market prices have not risen above eight cents a pound in the last two years and at one time fell to as little as two cents a pound. This represented a huge loss of income for the countries concerned.

The reduction in quotas between 1985 and 1986 has been estimated to have cost the Caribbean and Latin American region US$89.9 million in revenue.[6] In 1985 these countries formed themselves into a 'sugar group' to lobby the US administration to increase their quotas. One of the proposals they put forward was that the US should increase its sugar imports by one million tonnes for turning into sugar syrup. This would cut into the HFCS market but would not harm domestic sugar beet or cane production.[7]

But their plea had little effect. Congress slashed the import quota for the Caribbean by 25% for the 1985/86 crop year. The cut, from 1.7 million tonnes to 1.25 million tonnes took effect from December 1985 and there were further reductions in 1987.

Hardest hit is the Dominican Republic which holds the largest individual US sugar import quota. Sugar accounts for 40% of the country's foreign exchange earnings, half of which came from its US quota exports. The value

One of the countries hardest hit by US reductions in imports is the Dominican Republic.

of its US quota has declined from US$137 million in 1983/4 to only US$39 million in 1987. Its foreign exchange loss for 1986 alone was estimated to exceed US$50 million, all at a time when it needs to raise US$1 billion a year to pay off its foreign debt.[8]

The Philippines has also suffered. Its 1987 quota allocation of 143,000 tonnes is only a fraction of the 1.3 million tonnes it was exporting to the US during the 1970s. The value of its US quota in 1987 was a quarter of its value in 1983 and the quota is fully expected to be phased out altogether by 1990.[9]

Following the United States' 1964 embargo on trade with Cuba, the Philippines invested heavily in new mills and planted more sugar at the United States' request. Despite this, representations by the Government of the Philippines to Congress in 1986 for an increased quota have gone unheeded.[10]

Clearly, it is only a matter of time before the US stops all its sugar imports. Like a number of European countries, such as Britain, France and Holland, it has encouraged the development of cane industries in selected countries around the world to ensure a steady supply of sugar to its domestic market. In doing so it has also ensured their economic dependence on sugar. Now America no longer needs their exports, the Third World producers' only alternative is to sell their sugar on a depressed world market, with an inevitable loss in foreign exchange earnings.

Reduced income from sugar also reduces the ability of governments to meet payments on foreign debts, or import bills. Frequently they are forced to cut back on expenditure which often results in cuts in basic services – such as health and education – rising unemployment and higher food prices because of reduced subsidies. The impact of the United States' reduction in sugar imports on the Third World poor extends way beyond the cane fields.

ISOGLUCOSE

Although the United States is by far the largest world producer of isoglucose (High Fructose Corn Syrup) it is also produced in significant quantities in Canada, Japan and the EC, in smaller quantities in several non-EC European countries and in a few countries in Asia, Latin America and Africa.

In Canada the market for corn sweeteners has been growing rapidly. By 1984 they accounted for one third of the total sweetener market. The production of isoglucose only began in 1979 but is already taking a sizeable proportion of the sweetener market. Sugar consumption has been declining steadily, from 81% of total sweetener consumption in 1981 to 64% in 1985.[11]

Japan imports nearly two million tonnes of sugar a year for which it pays the highest sugar support prices in the world.[12] As a cheaper alternative they are currently trying to find a way of producing isoglucose from domestically grown rice. Once this is achieved they will be able to cut back on their sugar imports, most of which come from Australia, Cuba, the Philippines, South Africa and Thailand.

The chances of isogluose gaining ground in the European market look remote despite the EC's 16.5 million tonne wheat surplus, which could provide the raw material. The combined power of the sugar beet and refining lobby has ensured that its production is kept in check.

In the late 1970s, when it became apparent that starch producers in the EC wanted to go into isoglucose production to help relieve their over-capacity problems, the Community started to control production. Their justification for doing so was that there was already a structural surplus of sugar in the Community, and that the production of a cheaper substitute to replace sugar in important food and drink uses would only increase the surplus. In 1981 isoglucose was incorporated into the sugar regime and its production limited to 198,000 tonnes dry matter.[13]

THE WAY FORWARD

The reality that has to be faced by beet and cane producers is that high fructose syrups are here to stay. There is little doubt that they will continue to expand their share of the world sweetener market, particularly once the commercial production of granulated isoglucose is viable. Already it has been projected that by 1990 isoglucose will account for about one tenth of the world sweetener demand, and 45% of the US market.[14]

The displacement of cane imports from the US market has already caused immense hardship in developing countries like the Philippines and the Dominican Republic. The continued expansion of the industry is likely to have a similar impact on other developing country cane exporters unless

Coke — now sweetened with maize instead of sugar.

steps are taken to avoid this happening. There are two ways in which their interests could be protected; first by paying them compensation for the loss of their export markets, and second by establishing controls over the production of isoglucose.

The National Federation of Sugar Workers, the principal Philippines' sugar workers' trade union, has requested payments of US $2.5 million each, from Coca Cola and Pepsi Cola, to compensate the sugar workers for the disruption to the industry caused by the contraction of the US market.[15] If the companies agree to pay, the money will be spent on converting the land to food production. Had compensation been paid when the US first began cutting the Philippines' export quota, at least some of the suffering experienced by the people of Negros might have been avoided.

The need to control the production of isoglucose is a compelling argument for incorporating all alternative sweeteners, including isoglucose, into the International Sugar Agreement. The volatility and instability of world sugar prices stem from the 'free' market structure for sugar. The displacement of cane from its traditional markets by the establishment of isoglucose industries has led to increasing amounts of sugar being traded on the world market and the consequent fall in prices. The inclusion of all major forms of sweetener production, whether traded or not, into an International Sugar Agreement is necessary, therefore, to ensure some order in the world market place.[16]

SWEET NOTHINGS – SUGAR AND HEALTH

Sugar.... *"Yet being much used produceth dangerous effects in the body; as namely the immoderate uses thereof, as also of sweet confections, and Sugar-plummes, heateth the blood, ingendreth the landise obstructions, cachexias, consumptions, rotteth the teeth, making them look blacke, and withall, causeth many times a loathsome stinking breath. And therefore let young people especially, beware how they meddle too much with it."*
James Hart, Diet of Diseases, 1633.[1]

While Jamaican sugar workers despair over meagre wage packets, the major sugar producers squabble over market shares and scientists puzzle over how to make granulated sugar out of corn and other starches, many health professionals are waging war on a product that is widely claimed to be bad for us.

The problem with sugar is that it contains calories but little else. Furthermore, processed sugar tends to displace other foods from the diet because it causes a rapid rise in the blood-sugar level, which falls again, and causes hunger, even a craving, for more sweet foods. It thus sets up a dependency which drives out a natural desire for starchy and sweet wholefoods which supply blood-sugar at a normal rate, because that comes to feel too slow.[1]

Whilst many doctors and dentists claim that sugar is harmful to both teeth and health, it is the dental profession that is most united in its condemnation. The majority of dentists accept the evidence that sugar is the principal cause of dental caries – a disease that affects over 95% of dentate adults in Britain.[2]

The medical view is less united. Sugar has been cited as a major contributor to many conditions including obesity, diabetes, heart disease, cancer of the bowel and kidney stones, but there is disagreement on whether it is a direct or indirect cause of these.

The British Medical Association recently launched an attack on sugar consumption.[3] In the interests, at least, of dental health the BMA recommends that sugar consumption be halved, and targets confectionery, soft drinks and snacks as the main foods where this reduction should take place.

The sugar industry in Britain has its own counter-offensive to the health lobby. The nerve centre of their publicity operation is the London based British Sugar Bureau (BSC). The Bureau is jointly financed by Tate and Lyle and the British Sugar Corporation. Its Director General is MP Michael Shersby who is also Chairman of the Conservative Party's Food and Drinks sub-committee.[4]

The British Sugar Bureau's booklet **Sweet Reason** attacks the 'myths' expounded by the dental and medical professions.[5] They maintain that there are many causes of dental decay, sugar being one of them. As for other charges concerning sugar's culpability for obesity, heart disease and diabetes the BSC informs doctors that, "There is no evidence available to suggest that sugar-containing foods make any negative contribution to the diet of man."[6] In 1984 the British Sugar Corporation launched a £1,000,000 advertising campaign "to give sugar its proper recognition".[7]

Cane better than beet?

On health grounds it is frequently argued that policies should aim at reducing sugar consumption world-wide.[8] By implication production should also be reduced. This bodes ill for cane and beet industries alike, although recent evidence on the health front could possibly be good news for the cane producers.

Professor John Yudkin, author of **Pure, White and Deadly** and champion of the anti-sugar lobby, has recently completed a research programme into the properties of unrefined molasses sugar. His findings show that it contains certain important minerals which are not found in refined sugar. Principally these minerals are iron, zinc and chromium together with small quantities of calcium, magnesium and potassium. "Sugar is still bad", the report concludes, "but unrefined sugar is much less bad than refined sugar".[9]

The good news for developing country producers is that unrefined sugar comes exclusively from cane sugar. The molasses derived from beet is inedible unless refined because of its strong, bitter taste.[10]

Sweet Alternatives

Options for cane producers

'The noisy call for diversification should not divert people's attention from the real problems of landlessness and low wages which are at the root of widespread poverty and hunger in the countryside.'

Joel Rodriguez — Executive Director, Forum for Rural Concerns, Philippines

Chapter 7

FOR MANY DEVELOPING COUNTRIES growing sugar for export has become a liability, rather than an asset. The United States no longer needs their exports. The European Community is producing huge surpluses of beet. Major developing country producers, such as Cuba, Thailand, India and Brazil, have expanded production, and others have endeavoured to increase their self-sufficiency in sugar. Traditional markets have contracted, and the world market is so overloaded with surplus sugar that prices have fallen way below the cost of production.

Yet their need for foreign exchange is great. The 1970s oil price rises and subsequent increase in bank lending left many developing countries deeply in debt. They now face considerable pressure to repay their loans, from banks, the International Monetary Fund, whose policies are largely determined by Western Governments, and other lending institutions. They are encouraged to increase export earnings but find it increasingly difficult to do so because of the general depression in world commodity prices. Many cane producing countries are encumbered with an industry that can no longer meet their pressing need to increase foreign exchange earnings. Yet large numbers of people depend on the industry for their livelihood.[1]

In looking for ways round this problem various options are being tried by different countries. These fall into three main categories: diversifying out of sugar in order to grow either alternative cash or food crops; developing alternative uses for sugar; and reducing dependence on traditional markets by exploring the possibility of setting up alternative marketing arrangements or cane refining facilities.

DIVERSIFICATION OF LAND USE

Diversification, which in this context means substituting alternative cash or food crops for sugar, is an option that is being taken by a number of developing country sugar producers.

The Philippines

Following the crisis in the sugar industry which led to such widespread suffering on the island of Negros, considerable efforts are being made to diversify out of sugar.

The experience of Negros has been a salutary lesson in the risks of relying too heavily on one export crop. Agriculturally there is no need to grow sugar on Negros. Its rich soils and tropical climate mean that a variety of crops, such as rice, sweet potato, cassava and pineapple, could be grown there.[2]

Whilst meeting the food needs of the island's population must be the priority concern, the Philippines is also under tremendous pressure to generate foreign exchange. It has an external debt of US $26 billion (£17.5 billion) and an annual debt repayment bill of US $2 billion, almost half its foreign exchange earnings.[3] A diversified farming system, therefore, that includes food crops and a number of different export crops, is seen as a necessary safeguard against adverse market fluctuations, as well as providing food and employment.[4]

However, attempts to diversify are being hampered both by a lack of capital and the present land ownership structures. This has given rise to demands for land reform and the payment of compensation by the United States for cutting its import quota.[5]

The Caribbean

Most of the Caribbean islands import food partly because their populations are too large to be supported by domestic agriculture and partly because sugar and other export crops have taken up much of the best land. Cane is easy to grow, and is particularly well suited to the climatic conditions of the region.

In order to avoid stiff competition from larger producers several islands have switched from sugar to banana production. But the banana business has proved to be just as risky. Like sugar, bananas suffer adverse price fluctuations on the international market. They are also highly vulnerable to disease and to the region's frequent droughts and hurricanes.

In the Windward Islands nearly half the working population depend directly or indirectly on the banana industry. On occasions, when the area has been hit by tropical storms, there have been huge crop losses. In 1986, for example, Oxfam made a grant to the banana growers on the island of St Vincent because their crops had suffered severe damage during a hurricane.[6]

In recent years Jamaica has attempted to diversify some of its land out of sugar. As sugar became less productive, the island was under pressure from the International Monetary Fund to switch to alternative cash crops. Like the Philippines, Jamaica has a substantial external debt and a pressing need to generate foreign exchange.

Its diversification programme, partly financed by aid from the United States, commenced in 1984/85. The programme has several different components, a major one of which concentrated on winter vegetable production. Employing sophisticated technology it was designed to produce green peppers, cucumbers, cantaloupe melons, and other vegetables for export to the USA.

In 1986 the vegetable project was declared bankrupt and closed down. It

Harvesting green peppers in Jamaica for export to the USA.

had been unable to recoup its huge capital outlay because of depressed market prices in the United States.[7] In addition, it was poorly sited on the low-lying plains of the south of the island, which meant that flooding in the summer of 1986 caused severe damage to the crops.[8]

The project was unpopular from the outset with many sugar workers. It took on mainly casual labour because of the short harvest season, so many sugar workers were displaced and unable to find employment. Most of the project workers were women, drawn from neighbouring settlements, who would normally make a meagre living out of 'higgling', trading local produce in markets or on the road side.[9]

The irony is that in 1986 Jamaica had to import some 40,000 tonnes of sugar because it no longer had sufficient land in cane to meet its domestic and export requirements.[10]

Clearly, diversification programmes must be a priority in countries where the food needs of the population are not being met and the land in sugar is needed for the production of food crops.

The picture is far more complicated when the diversification is from sugar to alternative cash crops. In recent years most commodities have suffered from fluctuating and depressed world market prices which makes it almost impossible to choose a crop that will guarantee an improved income. An additional factor is that sugar is easy to grow in comparison with many other tropical crops, and much less likely to be damaged by pests and adverse weather conditions.

Although the situation varies greatly from country to country the success of any diversification programme depends on three main factors. Firstly, when diversifying to an alternative cash crop, it must be possible to select a crop, or crops, that are both climatically suited to the country concerned and reasonably assured of a stable export market. Secondly, whether the diversification is to cash or food crops, the capital required to diversify must be available. Finally, in all diversification programmes, there should be a commitment by governments to ensure that local farmers and sugar workers are fully consulted and integrated into the programme.

ALTERNATIVE USES FOR CANE

To cut down on the high costs of importing oil, and to make use of their sugar, a number of developing countries have started converting sugar into fuel alcohol, most commonly known as ethanol.

Sugar cane is particularly efficient at converting sunlight into chemical energy. It also produces its own fuel for processing, in the form of bagasse, the fibrous cane which remains after the cane juice has been extracted to make sugar. Its use as the base material for ethanol became particularly attractive in the 1970s when the rise in oil prices forced many developing countries to explore ways of reducing their dependence on imported oil.

Brazil has the world's largest ethanol programme. It first embarked this as a way of making use of its excess sugar. However, a spectacular rise in oil prices in the late 1970s led to a second boost to the programme in 1979 as the replacement of imported oil became a priority.

In all, US $8 billion has been invested in Brazil's 'Pro-alcool' programme. Substantial government subsidies to the programme have helped it to reach its present production of 3 billion gallons of ethanol each year. About 2.3 million cars, one third of the country's total, run on ethanol produced by Brazil's 386 sugar distilleries. 95% of new cars are equipped with alcohol burning engines.[11] Since it first started, the programme has halved Brazil's oil import bill.[12]

The picture has looked less rosy since the fall in oil prices in 1986. A barrel of petrol produced in Brazil from imported oil now costs less – at about US $25 – than a barrel of ethanol (about US $40).[13] Despite the changed economics there remains a strong lobby to maintain the 'Pro-alcool' programme, although there are others who consider there should be some serious rethinking.[14] In particular the programme has been criticised on the grounds that its social and environmental costs are unacceptably high.

Most critics agree that the main sectors to benefit have been the car industry, industries supplying equipment to the distilleries and the large landowners. It has also benefited the minority of the population rich enough to afford cars. But the programme has, at best, had little impact on the poor majority and at worst, harmed them. Small agricultural producers have been forced off their land by the expansion of cane production, and poor consumers are having to pay higher prices for food, partly due to the 'Pro-alcool' programme.[15]

About 2.3 millions cars in Brazil run on ethanol extracted from sugar cane.

Jenny Matthews-Format

Bringing sugar to the factory, Brazil.

In order to produce enough sugar for the programme, some 17 million hectares of land have been turned over to cane production.[16] This has involved the epxulsion of many small farmers from their land which in turn has led to a reduction in basic food production.[17] In the state of Pernambuco, for example, it is estimated that between 1975 and 1979 around 10,000 hectares of subsistence food crops were lost to cane.[18] In Brazil small farmers (with plots ranging from 1 to 100 hectares) are responsible for 60% of national food production, particularly of rice, beans, maize and cassava which form the basic diet of the majority of the population.[18] The reduction in the production of these crops has led to food price rises in many areas. These hit poor people hardest as they spend a high proportion of their income on food.

One expected benefit of the ethanol programme was increased employment. An estimated 800,000 new jobs have been created in the agricultural and industrial sectors.[20] In the original objectives of the programme it was stated that regional income differences would be reduced, since it is possible to produce the raw materials for alcohol production all over the country. It was also suggested that by locating plants in areas of high unemployment, local people would benefit directly.[21]

However, a study of the programme in 1978 showed that more than half the plants had been located in the comparatively industrially advanced state of Sao Paulo.[22] In addition to this, wages in many parts of the industry are extremely low.[23]

Environmentally the most serious consequence of the development of the

'Pro-alcool' programme has been water pollution. For every litre of alcohol produced there are approximately 12 litres of effluent which, if allowed to flow into water in high concentration, is fatal to fish and marine life.[24]

Oxfam supports a number of projects which work with the fishing communities around the cane growing regions.[25] As one project worker commented, "Ten years ago the river Golana was famous for the huge variety of fish, crabs and shrimps. People came from all around to fish, from the country and the surrounding towns and cities ... The river was a real breeding ground, and a fisherman could catch up to 30kg a day."

Today the situation is completely different. The subsistence fishing communities and unemployed of the region can no longer be sure of catching anything apart from illnesses from the highly polluted water of the Golana river, north of Recife.[26]

In one incident in August 1983 almost 1.4 billion litres of effluent from three distilleries were poured into two rivers in the state of Pernambuco. This caused severe damage to the rivers, estuaries and sea. A huge mass of polluted water, some 40km by 500m, spread along the coast. It is estimated that some 50 tonnes of fish were lost, along with shell fish and other marine life.

The effect on the poorer people who depend on fishing for their survival was disastrous. Whilst laws exist to reduce effluent, the fines are so low that companies consider it more economic to pay the fines than to install filtering equipment or treatment plants.[27]

Brazil produces more sugar than any other single country in the world. Despite the fact that its ethanol programme soaks up 60% of its sugar production, it still exports more than two and a half million tonnes of sugar each year. Rather than cutting back on exports, Brazil has merely expanded production which implies that developing alternative uses for sugar is not necessarily going to be the answer to the world's sugar surplus.

A number of other developing countries have ethanol programmes. For example, in Africa, Kenya, Zimbabwe and Malawi have operational ethanol plants. Of the three, Zimbabwe's programme appears to have been the most successful. It has had a positive influence on the country's balance of payments and reduced its strategic dependence on imported fuels. More importantly from the perspective of the poor, Zimbabwe has prioritised food production. The expansion in sugar production does not seem to have adversely affected food supplies.[28]

Attempts are also being made to start ethanol production in Jamaica. The recent failure of the island's diversification programme may be an added incentive to do so. An ethanol programme could save the island's sugar industry and with it several thousand jobs.

REDUCING DEPENDENCE

A major problem for many developing country cane exporters is that their industries are geared around producing sugar for refining and consumption in Europe and the United States. In order to reduce their dependence on these markets they would need to develop their own refining capacities and seek out alternative trading partners.

Refining

Most developing countries do not have the capacity to refine their own sugar. In some countries, sugar is sold to the consumer in a semi-refined form or, after a limited amount of extra purification in the mill, as 'plantation whites'. In other countries the consumer demand is for high-quality refined sugar.

So although the demand for refined sugar will vary from country to country, producers without the capacity to refine their own sugar lose out on the potential profits and additional employment opportunities of exporting it ready-refined. It also leads to anomalies, as in the case of Mauritius.

All the cane sugar that is exported to the European Community under the Lomé Convention is refined in Europe. Each year Mauritius sends 500,000 tonnes of raw sugar to the UK for refining by Tate and Lyle. Approximately 80,000 tonnes of this same sugar is then sold back, in its refined state, to Mauritius, where it is either consumed locally or re-exported.

Mauritian sugar workers argue that this is an illogical arrangement. If they had their own refining capacity they would be able to refine the 80,000 tonnes themselves, which would provide more jobs and save the considerable transport cost involved. They would also be able to make use of the molasses extracted in the refining process which they are unable to under the present arrangement.[29]

The ability of many developing countries to develop their own refining capacity is restricted by the small scale of many national markets (which rules against the construction of bulk sugar port facilities) and the limited returns from sugar refining.[30] In addition, refining can be extremely costly unless it can be done on a large scale and the refinery can be added to an existing raw sugar factory so that it can use surplus bagasse as fuel.

However, under present market structures, the main obstacle is the absence of stable markets. It is doubtful that cane sugar would retain its share of the EC market if the Community lost its capacity to refine the 1.3 million tonnes. If the cane sugar were to be imported ready-refined existing European refineries would be forced to close and the producer countries would lose their most powerful allies. In addition, the high cost of transporting refined sugar would add substantially to export costs and make it difficult for the cane producers to compete effectively with beet on the international markets.[31]

These problems could be overcome if some of the smaller sugar producers, such as those in the Caribbean, set up regional refineries on a similar basis to that currently being suggested by the the Mauritian sugar trades unions.

Alternative marketing arrangements

Another way cane producers could reduce their dependence on developed country markets is to seek out alternative trading links with other Third World countries and develop South-South trade.

The heavy cost of debt servicing has meant that many countries are unable to meet the costs of imports because of a shortage of foreign exchange. This has led to an increase in the volume of 'counter-trade', the term used for an exchange of goods of roughly the same value between countries.[32] There are a number of countries which exchange sugar for other goods as the following table shows:

South-South trade in sugar, 1982/3
Countries Commodities traded

(1)	(2)	(1)	(2)
Brazil	Venezuela	sugar	oil
Philippines	China	sugar	tools/machinery
Pakistan	Iran	sugar/rice etc	oil
Tanzania	Mozambique	sugar/cocoa etc	coffee/tyres etc

Source: Third World Quarterly, Vol 8, No 3, July 1986

There are obvious advantages to counter-trade in terms of an expansion of market opportunities and savings on foreign exchange. However, the opportunities for developing counter-trade in sugar are diminishing. Rather than exploring ways in which to obtain sugar by bartering it for other goods as a way of saving foreign exchange, an increasing number of countries are endeavouring to become self-sufficient. One example of this is Sri Lanka.

The Sri Lankan Government is in the process of establishing a huge sugar complex which aims to produce 20% of the island's sugar requirements.[33] Sri Lanka currently imports about 95% of its sugar, so the scheme is intended to save desperately needed foreign exchange. Several foreign companies are investing in the scheme but it is also being supported by the British aid programme, which allocated more than £14 million to the project in 1985.[34]

The project has generated considerable controversy, as the land that is being converted to sugar production is already being cultivated by small farmers for food production.[35] Quite apart from this, such a substantial allocation of British aid money for the purpose of establishing a new sugar industry, at a time of substantial world surpluses, is questionable. It might have been more appropriate to explore opportunitiess for obtaining more sugar through counter-trade, which would have both saved foreign exchange and increased market opportunities for an existing sugar exporter.

There is no simple solution to the problems that face developing country sugar exporters. Each country faces its own set of problems so whilst the option to diversify may be right for one, ethanol production may be more appropriate for another.

Europe and the United States have a clear role to play in suporting those countries whose industries have been adversely affected by their agricultural policies, in whatever option they choose. However, in all decisions that are taken, the needs of poor people must be of paramount importance.

NEW MARKETS FOR SUGAR

Why has sugar consumption fallen in developed countries? Undoubtedly health education and the resulting trend towards more healthy living has had an impact on the amount of sugar eaten. According to the British Ministry of Agriculture, Fisheries and Food Household Expenditure Survey of 1981, purchases of packet sugar declined by 30% between 1971 and 1981, as people either kicked the habit or switched to artificial sweeteners that are less fattening or harmful to teeth.[1] However the fall in domestic consumption has been partly been made up for by the switch away from home cooking to convenience foods with added sugar. The following table illustrates this trend in France, Germany and Britain:

Proportion of sugar consumption used by manufacturers and the proportion sold at retail[a] (% of total domestic sugar use)

		Proportion used by manufacturers[b]	Proportion sold at retail
France	1970/71	53.5	46.5
	1984/85	63.2	36.8
Germany	1970/71	60.2	39.8
	1983/84	70.9	29.1
UK	1970/71	51.6	48.4
	1984/85	61.9	38.1

Notes: [a] Sales at retail are mostly for domestic use by consumers.
[b] Principally food manufacturers, but small quantities also to the chemical industry.

Source: Review of EC Sugar Market.
Report to the World Bank, by Simon Harris (1985).

The decline in sugar consumption in the industrialised countries can also be accounted for by the increased use of other sugars such as fructose, glucose, lactose, maltose and galactose. In the USA High Fructose Corn Syrup has cornered 30% of the sugar and sweetener market. Europeans, Japanese, Americans and Australians may be eating less sucrose – sugar made from beet or cane – but this does not necessarily mean that they are eating less sugar.

With sucrose consumption falling in many parts of the industrialised world, new markets are being sought. Sugar is one of the first foods to respond to a rise in income in low income countries. Consumption begins to rise when a country's gross domestic product reaches about US $400 a head and continues to rise until GDP reaches US $6,000 a head when it starts to decline.[2]

91

The biggest users of sugar in Third World countries are the subsidiaries of large multinational food and drink processing companies and include cake and biscuit manufacturers and the soft drinks industry. Soft drinks are probably the most important factor in the sharp increase in sugar consumption. In Mexico, on average, nearly five bottles of soft drinks are consumed per man, woman and child each week.[3]

In the Philippines transnational giants like Coca Cola and Pepsi have virtually wiped out all traces of indigenous beverages like *kalamansi* (local lime juice) and *buko* (coconut water). Even in the most remote areas Coke and Pepsi have become standard fare.

Coca-Cola went to the Philippines in 1927, teamed up with the local San Miguel Corporation – the exclusive franchised bottler of Coke – and now has 17 bottling plants in the country, selling six million pesos worth of soft drinks a year. But even that figure was doubled by Coke's rival Pepsi which reported one and a half billion pesos worth of sales.[4]

Numerous studies have shown that populations who have changed their diet from locally available agricultural products to manufactured and processed foods, particularly those containing sugar, have experienced increased dental health problems.[5] This is the experience of several Oxfam supported consumer organisations in the Philippines who are waging war on the 'Coca-colonisation' and influx of other 'junk' foods into their country, mainly through health education programmes in schools.[6]

Soaking up the Surplus

Reducing EC surplus beet production and taking steps towards an International Sugar Agreement that works

'So long as the market remains in the doldrums developing countries' cane exporters will suffer.'

Frank Downie, Chairman of the National Sugar Corporation, Jamaica.

Chapter 8

WHILST DEVELOPING COUNTRY SUGAR EXPORTERS may consider various options to overcome the problems that their industries face, responsibility for the present crisis in the world sugar trade lies largely with developed country producers. Having set up cane sugar industries to meet their own needs and established a market dependency in their former colonies, they have gone on to establish their own, very productive sugar and sweetener industries. High Fructose Corn Syrup has displaced cane imports from the US market and the EC has swamped the world market with its beet sugar exports.

REDUCING EC BEET SURPLUSES

If the terms of trade are to improve for developing country cane exporters the EC will have to take its share of responsibility for reducing world sugar surpluses by limiting its own exports. In order to do this it will have to cut back on production, or develop alternative uses for its excess sugar.

Cutting back on Production

The European Community currently generates each year some 3 to 4 million tonnes of sugar, surplus to domestic requirement. This sugar is exported onto the world market, making the EC the single largest world market exporter of sugar.

The EC has been under considerable pressure to reduce its exports because of the devastation they have caused to world market prices. But Europe's powerful sugar beet lobby has strenuously resisted cuts in production as a way of reducing the surplus. The present pricing and quota system is very much to its advantage and reducing production would be an unpopular move for the Commission to make.

When considering how production could be cut it is helpful to see how the surplus occurred in the crop year 1985. As the sugar 'mountain' shows (see illustration), 'A' quota sugar is equal to Community consumption requirements. This means that, after taking the imported ACP cane sugar into account, 1.3 million tonnes of 'A' quota sugar is surplus production. All of the 'B' quota sugar is surplus and a substantial quantity of 'C' sugar is also being produced. This means that a great many farmers would rather take

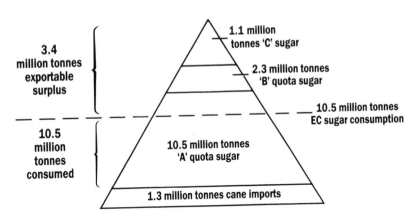

EC Sugar 'Mountain' 1
Crop Year (1985)

3.4 million tonnes exportable surplus

1.1 million tonnes 'C' sugar

2.3 million tonnes 'B' quota sugar

10.5 million tonnes EC sugar consumption

10.5 million tonnes consumed

10.5 million tonnes 'A' quota sugar

1.3 million tonnes cane imports

EC Sugar 'Mountain' 2

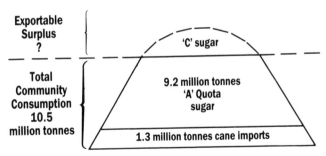

Exportable Surplus ?

'C' sugar

Total Community Consumption 10.5 million tonnes

9.2 million tonnes 'A' Quota sugar

1.3 million tonnes cane imports

the risk of producing 'C' sugar than have their quotas reduced because of their failure to meet them.

The obvious solution to this problem is shown in EC Sugar 'mountain ' 2. 'A' quota sugar has been reduced to 9.2 million tonnes which together with the 1.3 million tonnes of ACP imports makes up the total Community requirements for that year.[1] There is no longer a 'B' quota category, so all surplus sugar that is produced is unsubsidised.

Some factions within the Community argue that the easiest way of reducing exports would be to stop importing the 1.3 million tonnes of cane sugar from the ACP countries. However, this would amount to complete disregard for Europe's historical responsibility to the ACP countries' sugar industries and spell disaster for the countries involved. Whereas beet can be easily replaced by other crops, cane cannot.

The EC will review its Sugar Regime in December 1987 so that a new one can come into effect in July 1988. Provided the political will exists, there are two ways in which the Community could seriously address its problem of surpluses by cutting back on production. Either, it could review its price support system to make it less profitable for farmers to produce beet, or it could restructure the quota system on the lines suggested in the diagram showing sugar 'mountain' 2. Neither option will be popular with the majority of the Community's beet producers.

Whichever option is chosen it is important that small farmers within the Community are not penalised. Any adjustments to the Sugar Regime should take their interests into account, for example by allocating the 'A' quota sugar on a maximum tonnage per farm basis.

Alternative Uses

Within the EC, developing alternative uses for sugar is a more attractive proposition than cutting back on production. It is more acceptable to the Community's beet producers for the very reason that it would mean that they would not have to produce less sugar. There are two possible uses for surplus beet; ethanol production and the chemical industry.

European interest in ethanol production arises from two pressures. Firstly, the Community is committed to phasing out lead in petrol and the octane lost in this process could be replaced by ethanol. Secondly, the EC is under pressure to reduce beet surpluses which adds to the incentive to produce ethanol.

France is already a substantial ethanol producer using a wide range of products. These include imported molasses, alcohol distilled from wine, and sugar beet, which provides roughly one fifth of total production. The quantity of beet currently going for ethanol production is 1.26 million tonnes a year.[2]

At this stage the Community's position on ethanol production is not clear. Ethanol production will require large and continuing subsidies and the Commission is cautious about making any commitment to an extensive programme.[3]

Ethanol is only one of several possible alternative uses for sugar. Biotechnological advances have meant that there is an increasing role for sugar in the chemical industry. The European Commission has made much of this as one of its justifications for not cutting production quotas.[4]

It is forecast that the chemical industry could be using up to 539,700 tonnes of beet sugar by 1990.[5] This, however, depends on sugar being made available to the industry at a competitive price. Chemical manufacturers argue that in order for new activities to flourish in the EC, the industry must have access to the raw materials at remunerative prices, which the producers maintain are too low. Clearly, there is some way to go before the future of sugar in the chemical industry is clear.

As the chemical and ethanol industries are unlikely to be able to absorb four million tonnes of sugar a year, at least in the forseeable future, the EC will have to address the problem of reducing its surpluses by cutting back on production. The need for European action is pressing as its current lack of restraint in controlling exports is a major reason why recent International Sugar Agreements have failed to control world market prices.

INTERNATIONAL SUGAR AGREEMENTS (ISA) – THE FIRST FIVE

Before the 19th century, when trade was mainly between mother country and colony a system of tariffs was sufficient to foster production and keep other countries out of the home markets. When trade became international any move towards regulation had to have international agreement and recognition.

1864 – A few countries got together to try and draw up some kind of agreement on the sugar trade. It failed but this marked the first attempt to set up an international sugar agreement which would stabilise prices by controlling the movement of sugar around the world.

1937 – The International Sugar Agreement emphasised the need to maintain "an orderly relationship between supply and demand for sugar in the world market" and sought to maintain prices at a level which would ensure producers some degree of profit. An International Sugar Council was established to administer the Agreement.

During the Second World War sugar was in short supply and was rationed by many of the importing countries including the US and the UK. With the removal of wartime controls sugar prices fell dramatically and reawakened interest in a new ISA.

1953 – A third International Sugar Agreement was introduced. It had a broad array of aims which included the need to:

- balance supply and demand at equitable and stable prices;

- increase consumption;

- maintain the purchasing power of areas dependent on sugar production or exports;

- maintain fair labour standards.

To achieve this it set export quotas as a proportion of Basic Export Tonnage (BET) which were negotiated and reflected a combination of the reality of the market and the ideal. It also attempted to stabilise prices by setting prescribed price ranges.

The 1953 ISA kept prices within the prescribed range until 1957 when they soared because of crop failures and speculation associated with the Suez crisis. The Agreement was re-negotiated in 1958 and modelled closely on its predecessor.

1958 – International Sugar Agreement. Prices remained slightly below the bottom of the price range but it was the United States' reaction to the Cuban revolution that really damaged the credibility of the Agreement. At a stroke Cuba lost half its export market for sugar, and the US a third of its supplies. This altered the existing pattern of world trade as both countries sought markets and suppliers elsewhere.

Although both the USSR and China undertook to take all Cuban sugar displaced from the US market, the net result was more sugar coming on to the free market in 1960/61 than could be readily absorbed. This, combined with a large European beet crop in the same period, caused prices to fall to 2 US cents per pound – well below the prescribed price range. The economic provisions of the Agreement were allowed to lapse and no new agreement was negotiated to replace it.

1968 – The next International Sugar Agreement with economic provisions. This coincided with an upturn in world market prices largely due to a growth in consumption. In 1973 the price averaged 9.7 US cents per pound which made the ceiling of the supply commitment price of 7.6 cents per pound look both unattractive and unrealistic to exporters and the Agreement was not renewed at the end of the year.[1]

THE NEED FOR AN EFFECTIVE INTERNATIONAL SUGAR AGREEMENT

Attempts to control world commodity prices are usually made through international agreements. In other words, countries importing and exporting a specific commodity agree to buy and sell to one another within a fixed price range. Successive International Sugar Agreements, which incorporate both beet and cane sugar, have attempted to control world prices. However, in recent years these Agreements have failed to work.

Why the Sweet Talk has failed

The present International Sugar Agreement (ISA) contains no provision for controlling world prices. It commenced in January 1987, when it was signed by 55 sugar exporting and importing countries, but is purely an administrative agreement.[6]

Few previous ISAs have been completely successful in controlling prices. Nonetheless there have been periods when they have had some effect and their very existence has represented an important principle of trade co-operation between countries. The problems that led to the complete failure of the present agreement began in the 1970s.

During the 1970s there was a restructuring of world sugar trade. High world market prices for sugar early in the decade led to an increase in production in the exporting countries. These supplies came on stream just as world demand for sugar was declining and contributed to a dramatic fall in prices after 1974. At the same time the pattern of international trade was changing. In 1975 the US failed to renew its Sugar Act, which had been in existence since 1948. The expiry of the Act transformed the US sugar market from conditions of strict regulation to a relatively free market. In Europe, the Commonwealth Sugar Agreement was replaced by the Sugar Protocol of the Lomé Convention, which only permitted sugar imports from developing country producers.[7] These changes encouraged the establishment of a new International Sugar Agreement.

The International Sugar Agreement – 1978 to 1984

The new ISA, which commenced in January 1978, was the sixth of its kind. Like most previous Agreements it was originally set for a period of five years. However, before it expired it was decided to renew it for a further two years, which meant that it ran until the end of 1984.

The Agreement was negotiated against a background of high stocks and low prices, but there were other factors which also had a profound influence on the negotiations. Firstly, the United States, which had failed to participate in the 1968 ISA became an active and influential member of the 1977 Agreement. Secondly, the EC opted not to join the Agreement. Led by France it wanted to use the world sugar market as a means to avoid keeping its excess sugar in stock and did not want its programme of expansion to be limited by a quota system. Thirdly, Cuba wanted to increase its share of the world market. It had plans to expand output to 10 million tonnes. In addition the USSR had announced plans to achieve self-sufficiency in sugar. This would either have meant that Cuba would have had to reduce its exports to the USSR, or that the USSR would have become a major re-exporter of Cuban refined sugar.[8]

The traditional mechanisms of ISAs are export quotas, which were the basic instruments of the 1977 ISA. Additionally, in the 1977 ISA, exporting countries were expected to hold stocks of uncommitted sugar amounting to 2.5 million tonnes in total. These stocks were to be released onto the market gradually when prices rose above a certain level. Importing countries agreed to limit imports from non-members of the ISA. The prescribed price range was set at a floor of 11 US cents per pound and a ceiling of 21 US cents per pound. This was raised in 1980 to 13 to 23 cents per pound.[9]

The Agreement came into force in January 1978 when sugar prices were well below the bottom of the prescribed price range. They rose gradually as purchases were increased from the USSR and China. However, during 1980 there was a crop failure in Cuba. The reserve stocks were used up and the price of sugar rose sharply. Export restrictions were lifted but by the autumn of 1981 the price of sugar had fallen back to below floor level.[10]

It was decided to extend the Agreement for a further two years without re-negotiation even though it was clearly not succeeding in moderating price movements. Technical modifications which would have made it more effective were not made to the Agreement as countries had become dispirited by the EC's non-membership.

Negotiations for a New Agreement

From being a net importer in 1975, by 1981 the EC was exporting 5.3 million tonnes of sugar onto the world market. Such lack of restraint not only depressed world prices but also acted as a disincentive to ISA member countries to cut back on their own production. They took the view that this would only encourage further expansion by non-member producers such as the EC. As a result major sugar producers, such as Cuba, Brazil and Australia, urged the EC to participate in a new ISA.

The EC did participate in the negotiations for a new ISA and brought with it a proposal to replace the quota system of the 1977 Agreement with a system of so-called 'Reference Export Availabilities' (REAs). The REA was to represent a normal level of exports for each of the top ten exporting countries.[11] The total of REAs, plus a certain amount of exports from small or medium exporters were limited to between 20 and 21 million tonnes of sugar. If prices fell below a certain point the big ten exporters would be obliged to withhold from the market any stocks surplus to their REA.

Although other countries agreed to the idea in principle, they could not agree on the allocation of REAs, and this problem over market shares became a major sticking point. The talks finally broke down in June 1984 without any agreement having been reached and with sugar prices at a low of around 4 US cents a pound.[12]

The new ISA came into effect in January 1985. However, it did not contain any economic provisions to control prices, which means that it is purely an administrative agreement, to be re-negotiated after one year. It was designed as an interim measure as ISA members realised that until the big four sugar producers; Brazil, Cuba, the EC and Australia, could reach an agreement over market shares it would be impossible to implement an ISA with economic provisions.

Despite regular meetings during 1985 the four failed to come up with an agreement. In addition to the EC insisting on a larger market share, Australia is demanding guaranteed minimum export entitlement and Cuba wants its special agreement trade with the USSR to be fully accepted by Australia.[13] At the end of December 1986 the ISA was extended for a further year, as an administrative agreement.

WITHOUT AN INTERNATIONAL SUGAR AGREEMENT
WORLD PRICES FOR SUGAR DURING 1985 and 1986

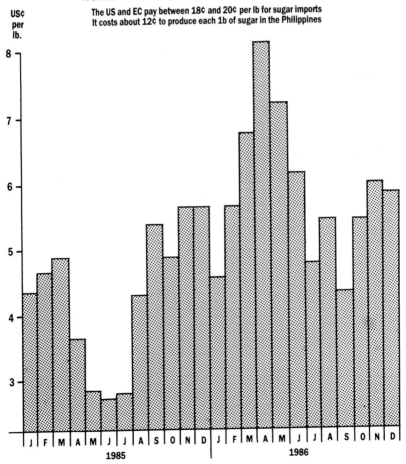

The US and EC pay between 18¢ and 20¢ per lb for sugar imports
It costs about 12¢ to produce each 1b of sugar in the Philippines

Source: Spot Prices, South Magazine   March 1985–February 1987

THE CASE FOR AN INTERNATIONAL SWEETENER AGREEMENT

Even if the EC, Cuba, Australia and Brazil do manage to sort out their differences and there is an ISA with full economic provisions it is unlikely to be effective. The problem is that the ISA is outdated.

International Sugar Agreements are designed to control the world prices of beet and cane sugar. The reality that the beet and cane producers face is that an increasing share of their market is being taken away from them by alternative sweeteners. Isoglucose has had the most significant impact in this respect. Projections are that, by 1990 it will account for one tenth of the world market for sweeteners.[14] This share is likely to become even larger once it is possible to market it in its dry, or granulated, form.

This change in market conditions will have to be coped with if world prices for sugar are ever to be stabilised. One way of doing this would be by incorporating all alternative sweeteners into the International Sugar Agreement and, in effect, transforming it into an International **Sweetener** Agreement. The Agreement could then provide a general and comprehensive framework in which to plan the marketing and production of all major forms of sweeteners.[15]

The immediate need is for an Agreement that will help be effective in controlling world market sugar prices. Whilst the ISA is no more than a token administrative agreement, sugar prices stand little chance of a recovery and those developing country cane producers that depend on the world market for a proportion of their sugar exports face considerable economic strain.

In search of a better deal

Improving conditions for sugar workers

'The future prosperity of the Dominican sugar industry, and the pace at which the conditions of the workers employed in that industry can be improved, will to a large extent be determined by its ability to sell its product at adequate prices on the world market.'

ILO Commission of Enquiry into the Dominican Republic's sugar industry, 1983.

Chapter 9

AS THE INTERNATIONAL LABOUR ORGANISATION (ILO) pointed out in the case of the Dominican Republic, workers' conditions are only likely to be improved once sugar exporters receive better prices. And yet the sugar industry has not always been in crisis. There have been many periods in its history when it has enjoyed considerable prosperity, but the benefits have rarely been shared with the workers. No amount of adjustment to world trade, therefore, can guarantee improved conditions for sugar workers.

At the root of the miserable conditions that sugar workers experience in many parts of the world is the system of production. It is often based on the plantation system which was first created in the tropical regions by colonial expansion to provide agricultural commodities, such as sugar.

Plantations were designed to maximise crop production but keep the costs as low as possible. Typically one crop was grown, and the work was done by slave labour. The slaves lived on the plantations which were designed to be self-contained so that the slaves had no life outside them. Whilst the owners generally accrued considerable wealth, the slaves were condemned to a life of poverty. After emancipation, slaves were replaced by paid workers who inherited much the same production system.[1]

Today much of the world's cane sugar is produced on plantations. In Jamaica they are known as 'estates' and in the Philippines as 'haciendas'. Whatever name they are known by, the basic structures are similar and, irrespective of market conditions for sugar, the workers are generally low paid, poorly housed and have very little or no land on which to grow food.

Not surprisingly it is sugar workers themselves who have been most vocal in their demands for improved working and living conditions. Their attempts to organise to improve conditions have often been brutally repressed.

Between 1981 and 1984 fifty-six sugar worker union organisers and leaders were assassinated in Brazil. One of these victims was Margarida Maria Alves. She was shot dead in August 1983 as she stood in the doorway of her home. As president of the Rural Workers Union of Alagoa Grande she had been directing a sugar workers' campaign to secure the minimum wage, an eight hour day, extra pay for overtime, adequate health care and control of small plots of land for food production.[2]

Members of the Philippines National Federation of Sugar Workers have suffered a similar fate. Many have been gaoled, tortured or murdered by the police or military forces. During the Marcos era union members were, at best, labelled 'subversive'. At worst, they were found beheaded in the cane fields – the fate of Rondolfo Golez, a 28 year old sugar worker from Negros who died in July 1985. According to ICCSASW his 'crime' had been to grow food on a tiny piece of land behind his house.[3]

Rally in Negros to demand land reform and improved working conditions.

OTHER WAYS OF PRODUCING SUGAR

The main problem with the plantation system is that it denies workers control over the land or means of production. Yet sugar cane is not only grown on plantations. There are a number of different ways in which it is produced, which do allow workers at least some degree of control. The following are examples of just three of these, illustrated by specific schemes; a cooperative programme in Jamaica, an outgrowers scheme in Kenya and efforts to bring about land reform in the Philippines.

Cooperatives

In a number of countries sugar is produced by cooperatives, in other words it is grown and harvested collectively, by the workers, who share the profits, or losses, of production. The short-lived cooperative programme in Jamaica illustrates some of the advantages of cooperative production over plantation production, but also some of the problems.

During the 1970s, in an attempt to improve conditions in the sugar industry, the governing People's National Party turned the ownership and management of Jamaica's three government owned sugar estates, Money-

105

musk, Bernard Lodge and Frome, (recently acquired from the British company Tate and Lyle and the US company United Fruits) over to the workers. The three estates were divided into twenty-six farms – each one forming a separate administrative unit which was run as a workers' cooperative.

The scheme lasted six years. Following a change in government in 1981 the cooperatives were dissolved and the new government resumed owner-ship and management of the estates.

In assessing the success or failure of the Jamaican cooperative scheme two criteria have to be taken into account. The first concerns their effect on the workers and the second the impact that they had on the financial health of the industry.

In terms of their impact on the workers, many of the people who were involved in the scheme look back on the days of the cooperatives with a sense of regret and loss. They felt that it was the one period in their lives when they were allowed a degree of responsibility, dignity and self-esteem. The education programmes that were organised to equip workers with the skills necessary to run the cooperatives meant that many of them became highly numerate and literate. They said that food was more plentiful because they had the land to grow their own, and for the first time they had some control over their own working lives.

At Frome Estate, where one of the first cooperatives was established, there is a small, red brick building which used to serve as the cooperative's community hall. The workers recall how it had been the centre of coopera-tive activity, the place where they used to put on shows, hold dances and have meetings. It now stands empty, having been taken over by the new management.

The sign-board of one of Jamaica's cooperatives at Frome Estates still stands.

106

They also recall the importance to them of a car that they bought with cooperative funds. It performed many different functions, acting as taxi to ferry their representatives to Kingston for meetings, ambulance, wedding car and funeral hearse. For the first time ever they were able to take their dead to the burial ground in dignity, and not by horse and cart or tractor. The loss of the car was felt acutely.

In the short period that they existed the cooperatives did little to improve the income of sugar workers. However, as many of the farms set aside land for food production, workers claim to have eaten better during the period. As one sugar worker said, "We may not have been rich but we never went hungry."[4] This land is now back under cane but a special source of discontent is that they are no longer allowed to graze their animals on fallow estate lands.

Yet none of the sugar workers romanticise the cooperative days. Many of them say that the changes which were required of them were tough and that there were times when they longed to go back to the old plantation system. As one woman said, "At least you knew who was who and what was what." But it is with deep regret that many of them look back on the days of the cooperatives, often blaming themselves for the failure of the scheme.

Whilst the morale of workers improved, the financial health of the industry suffered under the cooperatives. In the six years that the cooperatives were in existence, sugar production in Jamaica fell by a third and the volume of exports was halved.[5]

However, the cooperatives had inherited an industry which was already in serious decline. In the previous ten years, production had fallen by 15%. From accounting for one third of all exports, sugar was by then contributing only 10%. During each year of operation since 1965 the three estates had recorded a deficit.[6] Quite simply, the companies which preceded the cooperatives had run down the fields and infrastructure.[7]

From the outset the cooperatives had severe cash problems. They needed, but never received, capital to get them off to a healthy start. Instead they quickly accumulated considerable debts which remained on their books until they were dissolved in 1981. Their own cash problems were aggravated by the island's overall economic problems. Deeply in debt, the government was given little option but to devalue the Jamaican dollar. The more it did so the more difficult it became to obtain spare parts, fertiliser and other necessary inputs.

Another problem that beset the cooperatives was that whilst the fields were turned over to workers' control the factories remained under the old style of management. This aggravated existing tensions between field and factory workers – arising from slight differences in social status and living standards. Strikes, slowdowns and breakdowns plagued the industry and cut into harvest returns.

But the cooperatives faced more than financial problems. Such profound changes were bound to encounter difficulties. At government and administrative level there was considerable conflict about how the cooperatives should be run. At worker level there was also conflict. As one observer wrote

107

at the time, "the workers were used to taking orders, not giving them; they were constantly denigrating themselves and others like themselves; they felt little hope in the future, and they were prone to expect paternal-dependency relationships vis-a-vis those of a higher status and lighter colour."[8]

These attitudes, produced by years of conditioning, could not be changed overnight. To succeed, the cooperatives needed a great deal more time and money than they ever received.

Outgrowers Schemes

Only about half Jamaica's sugar is grown on plantation-style estates. The rest is supplied to the island's sugar factories by outgrowers. There are outgrowers schemes in many different cane producing countries. In some, such as Jamaica, they supplement the sugar grown on plantations. In others, such as Fiji, all the cane is supplied by outgrowers.

Outgrowers are farmers who grow sugar on their land as a way of generating a cash income. Sugar is likely to be one of a variety of crops grown. Many outgrowers set aside some of their land for food production, and may also grow other cash crops. The size of the farm, and thus the amount of sugar cane grown, varies considerably. The larger farm units often employ people to cut the cane. On the smaller farms the work is generally done by the family that owns the land.

The ability to generate a cash income is an important factor in alleviating rural poverty. The benefit of growing sugar, or any other crop, as a cash crop will depend on a number of factors; the amount the farmer is paid for the harvest, the cost of inputs – such as fertiliser – transportation costs and the availability and terms of loans.

There are numerous examples of outgrowers schemes. One example in Kenya, cited by the Intermediate Technology Development Group (ITDG), is the West Kenya Sugar Company (WKSC).[9] Because of its combination of small-scale factory production and an outgrowers scheme, ITDG feel that it is a good example of how sugar can make a positive contribution to rural development.

The company, which is situated in the Western Province of Kenya, is privately owned by a consortium of African businessmen. Its factory operates on a much smaller scale than most cane factories. It only produces about 20 tonnes of sugar products a day, compared to the larger factories which produce between 300 and 800 tonnes a day. ITDG helped design the equipment used to process the sugar cane. The technology used is deliberately designed to be labour, rather than capital, intensive. Western Province is an area of extensive underemployment, so according to ITDG the work that the factory generates is welcome.

Cane is supplied to the factory by outgrowers. The Company provides transport, interest-free credit and advice, whilst the farmers are responsible for ploughing, planting and weeding their own plots of land. This allows them a considerable degree of control over their land and as a result most of them also grow food crops. The company pays them the fixed government rate for the sugar that they sell to the factory.

ITDG feel that the scheme has been successful in that it has generated rural employment and improved the cash income of local farmers without adversely affecting local food production. They would like to see more schemes of this type set up in Kenya.

Land Reform

Outgrowers schemes are only possible if people own, or have access, to land. In the Philippines much of the land is owned or controlled by wealthy individuals or multinational corporations. Rural poverty is extensive because the vast majority of people do not have access to the land or lack the means to make it productive. Because of these inequalities there have been widespread demands for land reform.[10] For the sugar producing island of Negros this would involve dismantling the **hacienda** system by taking land away from the control and ownership of a few wealthy landowners, and redistributing it among the workers.

Land reform is regarded as essential by the National Federation of Sugar Workers (NFSW), the main sugar workers' union in the Philippines, if rural poverty is to be alleviated. They argue that as the current crisis in the industry has exacerbated existing suffering among sugar workers, the priority must be a fundamental restructuring of land-ownership. Under the present system, even if the terms of trade were to become more favourable, the workers would be unlikely to benefit.

The Union's Cooperative Farm Lots Programme, which is supported by a number of development agencies, including Oxfam, is an attempt to

Sugar workers discuss the Farm Lots programme.

109

diversify some of the land in Negros away from sugar into food production. It has involved organising workers to negotiate with the owners of the **haciendas** where they work, to secure an area of land for cooperative food growing. As sugar workers are not farmers they generally need training in subsistence farming. The scheme aims to provide the necessary training – in both food production and cooperative management – as well as providing revolving loans for inputs, such as seeds, fertilisers, tools and work animals.

The scheme has proved successful. By May 1986 some of the cooperatives were already harvesting food crops, and where this had happened conditions were improving. However, the main concern of the union was that, until land reform becomes government policy, the success of the scheme depends largely on the cooperation of the land owners. While world market prices were low, some were only too willing to loan a portion of land to their workers. The fear was that if prices rose there would be the danger that the landowners would exercise their power and convert the land back to sugar production.

As all three cases show, conditions for sugar workers cannot improve without the commitment of Third World governments to making structural changes in order to alleviate the more general problem of rural poverty. This may involve land reform, providing technical back-up, credit facilities or the necessary marketing channels so that farmers are able to sell their produce and thereby generate an income.

WAYS IN WHICH DEVELOPED COUNTRIES COULD SUPPORT EFFORTS TO IMPROVE CONDITIONS FOR SUGAR WORKERS

Although the onus of reform must lie with the governments of Third World producer countries there are a number of ways in which developed countries could support improvements in conditions for sugar workers.

Aid

In 1984 nearly £24 million of British aid money (more than half the total amount allocated to agricultural programmes) was used to finance Third World sugar projects. The amount was, admittedly, unusually high. In the following year, for example, only £500,000 was allocated in this way. However, the bulk of this expenditure, £14.3 million, went into financing the setting up of a huge sugar complex in Sri Lanka.[11] The complex is designed to help Sri Lanka become self-sufficient in sugar and save precious foreign exchange on imports. But the scheme also displaced a large number of peasant farmers from their lands and generated considerable controversy.[12]

Very often, as in the case of the Sri Lankan sugar project, aid is directed at promoting the economic growth of a country so that, in theory, the country as a whole benefits. However, in Oxfam's experience the benefits of this type of aid rarely reach the poor.[13] The Sri Lankan farmers, dispossessed of their lands, will now have to work on the sugar estates in order to earn a living. Once the project is established it may well be that they will face similar problems to sugar workers in the Jamaican estates or Brazilian plantations.

If aid is genuinely to benefit the Third World rural poor, and alleviate poverty among sugar workers, it should be directed towards promoting land reform, increasing and diversifying rural credit schemes – so that small-scale farmers can afford to buy seeds, irrigation systems, fertilisers etc. – and improving extension services so that poor farmers have access to improved methods of cultivation.[14]

Finance

A number of references have already been made to how the collapse in world sugar prices has exacerbated the problems that many Third World sugar exporters face with paying off their debts to Western bankers. The debt crisis has had a major influence on Third World government policies. Their pressing need for foreign exchange has often led to their taking measures, such as reducing government expenditure, ending subsidies on food and other basic products, and increasing the production of export, rather than food, crops. Inevitably the people who suffer most from such policies are the poor.

In Oxfam's experience, many of these structural adjustment measures work directly against the much more pressing need, to alleviate Third World poverty.[15] One reason why Jamaica's sugar cooperatives were dissolved was the island's urgent need to generate foreign exchange. Under pressure from the International Monetary Fund the government decided that its need for income from the industry would be best served by the old-style plantation system. The cooperatives were never given a chance to succeed and a scheme that could have substantially improved the quality of life for the sugar workers, was abolished.

The debt crisis has hindered rural development in many countries. There is an urgent need for Western governments to remove the burden of debt repayments by taking measures such as writing off a proportion of a country's debt, or reducing interest rates. It is also necessary to ensure that IMF austerity measures do not force the removal of food subsidies or lead to cuts in basic services, particularly health and education, which directly benefit poor people. Third World governments must be given the 'economic space' to prioritise social as well as economic developmment.

Trade

Much has already been said about the negative impact Northern agricultural policies have had on Third World cane exporters and how unfair terms of trade have accentuated poverty. Measures such as a reduction in EC beet surpluses and the resurrection of an International Sugar Agreement with some power to stabilise world prices are vital. But trading agreements could also be used to support efforts to improve conditions for sugar workers.

In recognition of the extensive poverty that exists among sugar workers, recent International Sugar Agreements have contained a clause to the effect that all members of the Agreement must ensure a decent standard of living for sugar workers.[16] The Agreement is signed by more than 50 countries, many of which are Third World cane exporters.[17]

However, the ISA, even before 1984 when it became an administrative agreement without economic provisions, has had very limited success in its principal objective of controlling world market prices. Whilst it is unable to be effective in this respect, it is powerless to have any influence over its members regarding workers' conditions.

It could be argued that the ISA has, nonetheless, set a precedent for the inclusion of fair labour standard clauses in sugar trade agreements. However, if they are to be effective it must be possible to monitor labour standards, and impose sanctions against member countries which abuse workers' rights.

A major difficulty lies in defining the standards that are to be applied. Whilst the goal must be a significant improvement in working conditions, some standards would have to be considered absolute – the same for every country – and others relative, to take into account the relative economic strengths and weaknesses of different countries.

Absolute standards should cover, among other things, freedom from forced labour and the right to organise into trade unions and negotiate for better conditions with employers. Relative standards would have to apply to factors such as wages. It would be a nonsense to set internationally applied minimum or maximum wage levels as the cost of living varies so greatly from country to country. A decent living wage for a European sugar beet farm worker, for example, would have to be considerably higher than the same for a sugar worker in the Philippines. To apply standards in this respect would require a series of national household surveys indicating to what degree the basic needs of workers are satisfied in respect of nutrition, health, housing and social welfare.[18]

The International Labour Code of the International Labour Organisation (ILO) already provides a basis for a minimum level of protection for workers. If all the conventions of the code were to be respected by its 150 member states, many of which are sugar exporters, workers would be guaranteed full rights to organise and negotiate; freedom from forced labour and discrimination in recruitment, promotion and working conditions; compensation in case of redundancy, sickness and occupational injuries; a 40 hour working week and three weeks of annual leave and some form of minimum wage. Women workers would be granted maternity leave with pay, child labour would be effectively prohibited and measures would be taken to protect workers against poisonous substances and other occupational hazards.

The ILO has its own system of monitoring which led to an enquiry in 1983 into the employment of Haitian workers on the sugar plantations of the Dominican Republic.[19] As a result of the enquiry a number of recommendations were made that could substantially improve the conditions of the workers. If this system were to be more extensively or specifically applied, for example as a condition of trade agreements, the opportunity would exist to ensure workers a better deal.

On the assumption that fair labour standard clauses could help to improve conditions for sugar workers there is a strong argument for their inclusion in all sugar trade agreements. However, there are also dangers in this approach, the most serious of which is the scope that it gives the importing countries for protectionism. If a fair labour standard clause was to be inserted into the Sugar Protocol of the Lomé Convention, for example, there is a very real danger that it would give the EC's powerful beet lobby an opportunity to argue for a reduction in the EC's cane sugar imports.

Given the size of the European beet surpluses, it is easy to imagine that the inclusion of such a clause might be supported as an excuse to cut off imports from 'bad' countries, whilst not increasing imports from 'good' countries.[20] While conditions are bad for sugar workers in many producer countries, they would be a great deal worse if Europe stopped importing their cane sugar.

As a pre-requisite, therefore, to the insertion of a fair labour standards clause into the Sugar Protocol, the EC must greatly reduce its beet surpluses and re-affirm its commitment to import the agreed quantity of 1.3 million tonnes of cane sugar. Overall there will have to be a substantial improvement in terms of trade before fair labour standard clauses in trade agreements can be used as a progressive, rather than protectionist measure, to improve workers conditions, and keep the issue of poverty firmly on the trade agenda.

SUMMARY AND RECOMMENDATIONS

Falling commodity prices and shrinking markets have hit Third World producers hard. In no case is this truer than in the sugar industry upon which about 12 million workers and their families depend for a livelihood.

Sugar faces a special set of problems. In recent years cane producers have found themselves in direct competition with European beet and North American corn syrup. Due to the high prices paid to farmers under the Common Agricultural Policy, the European Community now produces vast surpluses of beet sugar. These are dumped on the world market and have contributed to a dramatic fall in world sugar prices. In the USA an expansion in the production of isoglucose has meant that the US has reduced its cane imports to a fraction of their former level.

Many Third World governments are under considerable pressure to generate foreign exchange through export-led growth because of the debt crisis and the high interest rates charged on borrowing. This has led to increased competition from other producers and compounded the problem of contracting markets and low world prices. Many cane exporting countries are unable to meet even their production costs. They are encouraged to adopt austerity measures, including removal of food subsidies and reductions in basic services. Oxfam's concern is that it is the poor who are invariably hardest hit by these measures.

The problems faced by sugar workers are in many ways inseparable from those of the rural poor as a whole. They include landlessness, low wages, poor working conditions and lack of basic amenities or services such as clean water, health care and education. But sugar workers suffer additional hardships arising out of the seasonal nature of production which means that many have work, and income, for only part of the year. The present crisis in the industry has meant that in many countries there are even fewer employment opportunities and as a result poverty is increasing.

There are no simple solutions. In order to alleviate rural poverty the political will of Third World governments is crucial. However, there is much that 'Rich World' governments could do to assist. They can modify Northern agricultural policies and make other changes to improve terms of trade. They can also ease the burden of the debt crisis on Third World nations, and direct aid in ways that will encourage and support structural changes to benefit the poor.

PRIORITIES FOR THIRD WORLD GOVERNMENTS

1. **Diversify control over sugar production** to promote rural development through a redistribution of resources.

i. Implement land reform programmes.

114

ii. Replace the plantation system with more equitable forms of production such as cooperatives or outgrowers schemes.

iii. Ensure that producers receive stable prices for their sugar and have access to credit so that they are able to borrow what they need for production.

iv. Ensure that producers have access to basic amenities, health services and education programmes.

v. Encourage and support trade unions and collective bargaining.

2. Diversify land use to protect against adverse market conditions and improve food self-sufficiency.

i. Where the food needs of the poor are not being met the production of food crops should always take priority over sugar.

ii. Where the production of food crops does not have to be a priority, land use should be diversified to alternative export crops to ensure a balance of production and avoid over-dependence on any one crop.

3. Diversify markets to lessen dependence on traditional markets.

i. Seek opportunities for South-South trade through selling or bartering sugar for other goods or commodities.

ii. Develop refining capacities to increase market opportunities.

4. Diversify crop use.

i. Explore alternative uses for sugar supplies to maintain or increase rural employment opportunities and, in the case of ethanol, to reduce reliance on imported oil.

HOW RICH WORLD GOVERNMENTS CAN HELP

Trade

Goal: to improve the terms of trade for Third World cane producers through market access and price stabilisation and provide an incentive to improve workers' conditions:

i. The EC should reduce its beet surpluses.
The EC should amend its quota system to help reduce current surpluses which are depressing world prices. This can be done by reducing the amount of sugar that receives Community support prices.

ii. Protect existing markets for cane.
The EC should ensure continued access of cane sugar to the Community under the Lomé Convention by setting 'A' quota sugar at the level of Community consumption minus the 1.3 million tonnes of cane sugar imports.

iii. An International Sugar Agreement to stabilise world prices.
Major producers (particularly the EC, Australia, Cuba and Brazil) should reach an agreement on market shares so that progress can be made in

115

agreeing a new ISA to stabilise world prices.

iv. Regulate production of isoglucose and other alternative and artificial sweeteners.

Discussions should begin, aimed at incorporating all alternative and artificial sweeteners into a new ISA that will provide a comprehensive framework in which to plan the production and marketing of all forms of sweeteners.

v. Incorporate fair labour standards clauses into trade agreements to provide an incentive for Third World governments to improve workers' conditions.

Debt

Goal: to ease the burden of debt repayments to give Third World governments the 'economic space' to implement the above reforms and prioritise social development rather than having to pursue export-led growth strategies or enforce crippling austerity measures:

i. Reduce the burden of debt and high interest rates by lowering interest rates.

ii. Partially write off government to government debts of some of the poorest countries.

iii. Reschedule debts to allow longer periods for repayments of loans.

iv. Ease the IMF's handling of the debt crisis so that any economic adjustment that may be necessary does not force cuts in basic services, or other measures which adversely affect the poor.

Aid

Goal: To ensure that Third World cane producers are fully compensated for loss of 'Rich World' markets, and direct aid to poverty focussed programmes:

i. Compensate cane producers for loss of markets.

Rich world governments and manufacturers should accept responsibility for the human consequences of changes in marketing and trading policy by paying financial compensation to assist structural changes such as land reform and diversification programmes.

ii. Redirect aid to support Third World governments in their efforts to redistribute resources and adjust to shrinking markets.

Aid should be used to help governments who are promoting land reform, and support rural transformation such as the provision of basic services, credit facilities and technical assistance to small farmers. It should help cane producers adjust to shrinking markets by supporting diversification programmes, establishing refining capacity or developing alternative uses for sugar.

Notes and References

SUGAR

1. Hagelberg, G.B. (1985), **Sugar in the Caribbean: Turning Sunshine into Money,** The Woodrow Wilson International Center for Scholars, USA, page 31.

CHAPTER ONE

1. For a description of the Sugar Protocol of the Lomé Covention see Chapter 3.

2. Approximately 30% of the workforce in Jamaica are unemployed. See Coote, Belinda (May 1985), **Debt and Poverty – a case study of Jamaica,** Oxfam.

3. Nearly half of Caribbean households are headed by women.
Campbell, Frank A., **Window on Caribbean Women,** IDRC Reports Vol 15, Number 3, PO Box 62084, Ottawa, Canada K1G 3HG.

4. When I visited Frome Estate in February 1985 many of the women workers were suffering considerable discomfort from open sores on their hands where they came into direct contact with the fertiliser. They also complained of sores on other parts of their bodies, including their vaginas. The company has since switched brands of fertiliser and the women confirm that the new type causes them less discomfort.

5. National Federation of Sugar Workers, **Sugar: Honey For a Few, Blood and Sweat for Many,** EILER, PO Box SM 157, 2806 Metro Manila.

6. Lopez-Gonzaga, Violeta B. (1984), **The Sacadas in Negros: A Poverty Profile,** Research Notes Series No 1, La Salle Research Center, Bacolod, Philippines.

7. On September 20th 1985 the military opened fire on a crowd of sugar workers who had rallied in the town centre to demand cheaper rice and land on which to grow food. Twenty seven people were killed and many more injured. **Mr and Ms Magazine,** September 27th, 1985.

8. Personal interview – Negros April 1986

9. IAA – **Fundacao Getulio Vargas,** 17.3.87.

10. International Commission for the Coordination of Solidarity Among Sugar Workers, '300,000 Brazil Sugar Workers Seek International Solidarity.'

11. The exchange rate on March 9th 1987 was 28.26 cruzados to £1 sterling (**Financial Times**).

12. Melo, Mario Larcerda de, (1985), **Acucar e o Homen, Problemas Sociais e Economicos do Nordeste Canavieiro,** MEC – Instituto Joaquim Nabuco de Pesquisas Sociais, Recife, (Survey carried out by Nelson Chaves).

13. **Oxfam's Practical Guide to Selective Feeding Programmes** (1984). Oxfam Health Unit.

14. Ibid.

15. Instituto Brasileiro de Estatisticas, (1980).

CHAPTER TWO

1. The meeting was organised by The International Commission for the Coordination of Solidarity Among Sugar Workers (ICCSASW) and hosted by the National Federation of Sugar Workers (NFSW). The NFSW is the main sugar workers' trade union in the Philiipines. ICCSASW is an international sugar workers' coordinating body based in Canada. It is not a trade union but a special body established by different unions and federations of sugar workers in sugar

117

producing countries around the world. It carries out a number of tasks which include research into the production and marketing of sugar, and the situation of sugar workers around the world. It distributes and exchanges this information, promoting education, solidarity and a network of contacts. The meeting held in Negros was one of the regional meetings that ICCSASW organises annually.

2. The explosion occurred in the Somayya Organic Chemicals factory in December 1985, in the Maharashtra region of India.

3. For more information see Chapter 8.

4. Hobhouse, Henry (1985), **Seeds of Change – Five plants that transformed mankind**, Sidgwick and Jackson, page 43.

5. Deerr, N. (1949), **The History of Sugar , Vol I and II.** Chapman and Hall Ltd, page 116.

6. Hobhouse, Henry (1985),op.cit., page 44.

7. Ibid, page 59.

8. Saunders, M. (1984), "Towards a Sugar Health Policy", Unpublished MSC Thesis, Cranfield Institute of Technology, page 19.

9. Francis, Armet (1985), **The Black Triangle**, Seed Publications, page 62.

10. Mintz, Sidney W. (1985), **Sweetness and Power**, Viking Penguin, page 67.

11. Doyal, Leslie (1979),**The Political Economy of Health**, Pluto Press, page 86.

12. Deerr, N. (1949),op. cit.

13. Ross, Peter (1986), **Sugar – Sweet and Sour, A Commodity Study**, Australian Council for Overseas Aid, GPO Box 1562, Canberra, ACT 2610, Australia, Chapter One.

14. Hobhouse, Henry (1985),op. cit., page 63.

15. Feuer, Carl Henry (1984), **Jamaica and the Sugar Worker's Cooperatives**, Westview Press, USA. page 2.
Edquist, Charles (1985), **Capitalism, Socialism and Technology – a comparative study of Cuba and Jamaica**, Zed Press, page 57.

16. Feuer, Carl Henry (1984), op. cit., page 24.

17. See Chapter 10 for more information on Jamaica's sugar cooperatives.

18. See Chapter 3 for more information on the Sugar Protocol.

19. Personal interview with Jagdish Koonjul, Mauritian Embassy, Brussels, 20.2.86.

20. The National Federation of Sugar Workers, **Sugar: Honey for a Few, Blood and Sweat for Many.** EILER, P.O. Box SM157, 2860 Metro Manila and The National Federation of Sugar Workers, Bacolod City.

21. 1934 – Jones-Costigan Act established a quota system. 1954 – The Laurel Langley Agreement placed further restrictions on sugar imports. 1974 – The Laurel Langley Agreement was suspended.

22. National Federation of Sugar Workers, op. cit.

CHAPTER THREE

1. The National Secretariat of Social Action (NASSA) is a component of the Catholic Bishops' Conference of the Philippines. The results of their survey were sent to Oxfam on July 16th 1985.

2. **Negros Update – on the emergency, rehabilitation and development programme.** UNICEF – Manila 29 April 1986.

3. **The Guardian**, 26.9.86

4. **Oxfam Project PHL 70.**

5. UNICEF, op. cit.

6. Ross, Peter (1986), op. cit.

7. **The Lomé Negotiations** – CIIR Comment, 1984 (CIIR/84).

8. Gordon-Ashworth, Fiona (1984), **International Commodity Control – A Contemporary History and Appraisal**, Croom Helm/St Martins, page 167.

9. Laidlaw, Ken (1983), **The Sugar Protocol:Room for Improvement**, Lomé Briefing No 12, Liaison Committee of Development NGOs to the European Communities, rue de Laeken 76, 1000 Brussels, Belgium.

10. **Sugar, the European Community and the Lomé Covention,**(Feb 1983), EEC Directorate General for Information – DE19. page 12.

11. For the 1985 allocations see Chapter 5.

12. Harris, Simon (1985), **Review of the EC Sugar Market**, Report prepared for the World Bank, Washington DC, USA. page 60.
13. Laidlaw, Ken (1983), op. cit.
14. Gordon-Ashworth, Fiona (1984), op. cit., page 166.
15. See Chapter 6.
16. Ross, Peter (1986), op. cit.
17. Ibid, page 15.
18. See Chapter 9 for more information on International Sugar Agreements.

TATE AND LYLE

1. Doyal, Leslie (1979), **The Political Economy of Health**, Pluto Press, page 126.
2. Tate and Lyle Annual Report and Accounts 1986.
3. News from Transnationals Information Centre, London, Octavia House, 54 Ayres Street, London SE1 1EU.
4. Harris, Simon (1985), **Review of the EC Sugar Market**, Report prepared for the World Bank, Washington DC USA, page 59.
5. Tate and Lyle Annual Reports and Accounts 1985 and 1983.
6. Tate and Lyle Annual Report 1986.

SUGAR BEET

1. **Sugar Year Book 1985**, International Sugar Organisation.
2. **History of Sugar** – British Sugar Bureau Information booklet.

CHAPTER FOUR

1. Harris, Simon. Swinburn, Alan. Wilkinson, Guy (1983), **The Food and Farm Policies of the European Community**, Wiley. page 124.
2. Most beet processors in EC countries operate this mixed-pricing system. It is often argued, however, that this works against the interests of the farmers who cannot choose whether they produce 'A' or 'B' quota sugar.
3. Agra Briefing no 7 (June 1985), **EEC Sugar Policy and the International Market**, Agra, Europe (London) Ltd
The figures given are for a Community of 9, in 1976 and a Community of 10 in 1985 – following Greece's accession in 1981.
4. Harris, Simon (Dec 1985), **Review of the EC Sugar Market**, Report prepared for the World Bank, Washington DC, USA, page 24. and Sugar Year Books 1985 and 1977 – International Sugar Organisation. (all figures shown are in raw sugar value.)
5. **Financial Times**, 2.10.85, Ivo Dawnay, "EEC Sugar Policy in Disarray".
6. Harris, Simon (Dec 1985), op. cit.
7. **The Economist**, 10.8.85.

CHAPTER FIVE

1. Harris, Simon,(Dec. 1985), **Review of the EC Sugar Market**, Report for the World Bank, Washington DC, USA, page 55.
2. Hagelberg, G.B.(1985), **Sugar in the Caribbean: Turning Sunshine into Money**, The Wilson Center, Smithsonian Institute Building, Washington DC.
3. Harris, Simon, op. cit., page 55.
4. Sutton, Paul (ed) (1986), **Dual Legacies in the Contemporary Caribbean**, Chapter – "The Sugar Protocol of the Lomé Convention", Frank Cass, London.
5. Ibid.
6. World Bank, **World Development Report 1986**, Oxford University Press , page 142.
7. Tate and Lyle Annual Report and Accounts, 1986.
8. Tate and Lyle, (1986), **A Unified Sugar Industry for Britain**.
9. Early Day Motion, No. 339, January 1987 (Amended). In a letter to Oxfam, Sir Richard Butler, chairman of AGRICOLA (UK) Ltd a subsidiary of the Italian firm Gruppo Ferruzzi, whose

competing bid with Tate and Lyle for ownership of British sugar was rejectedby the Monopolies and Mergers commission on 25.2.87, declared his support of British Sugar's stated commitment to maintain a UK cane refining industry: "..should Tate and Lyle decide to cease operations in the UK (a decision we would regret), Gruppo Ferruzzi will support British Sugar's declared willingness to process all cane sugar to which the European Community is committed." (19.2.87)

10. The Economist, 10.8.85.
11. Financial Times, 7.11.85.
12. Ibid.
13. Daily Telegraph, 18.8.84.
14. Herald Tribune, 10.7.86.

ALTERNATIVE SWEETENERS

1. Sanderson, M (1984), "Towards a Sugar Health Policy", unpublished MSC Thesis for Cranfield Institute of Technology.
2. Hagelberg, G B (1985), **Sugar in the Caribbean – Turning Sunshine into Money**, The Wilson Center, Washington DC, USA , page 24.
3. Harris, Simon (1985), **Review of the EC Sugar Market**, Report to the World Bank, Washington DC, page 69.
4. GATT-Fly (1980), **Corn vs Cane – the high fructose challenge**, 11 Madison Avenue, Toronto MR 2S2, Canada.
5. Thomas, Clive.Y (1985), **Sugar – Threat or Challenge?**, IDRC -244e, page 31.
6. New Scientist 19, June 1986, "The Shape of Sweeteners to Come", Leslie Howe and John Emsley.
7. The Guardian, 5.3.87.

CHAPTER SIX

1. Sweetener Analysis, January 1987, Landell Mills Commodity Studies.
2. St Paul Pioneer Dispatch, 4.10.86.
3. Thomas, Clive Y (1985), op. cit., page 43.
4. F.O. Lichts' **International Sugar Report**, Vol 118, No 30, 27 October 1986.
5. Sweetener Analysis, January 1987, Landell Mills Commodity Studies.
6. Daily Gleaner, 28.1.86, "US$90m sugar loss looms for Caribbean".
7. Financial Times, 22.8.85, "Caribbean producers ask U.S. to buy more sugar".
8. Washington Report on the Hemisphere, Jan 22nd 1986, Vol 6, No 8.
9. Manila Times, 15.5.86, "Bigger sugar quota sought".
10. Financial Times, 10.7.86.
11. Thomas, Clive Y (1985),op. cit., page 49.
12. Ibid, page 52.
13. Harris, Simon, (December 1985), op. cit.
14. Thomas, Clive Y (1985), op. cit., page 127.
15. Guilty of Hunger, (1987) COLA ACTION, 2e Wetieringplantsoen 9, 1017 ZD Amsterdam, The Netherlands.
16. Thomas, Clive Y (1985), op. cit., page 131.

SWEET NOTHINGS – SUGAR AND HEALTH

1. Canon, Geoffrey, "Bad Blood", **New Health**, May 1984.
Davidson and Passmore, **Human Nutrition and Dietetics**, Eighth edition, EL/BS 1986, page 197.
2. Sheiham, Aubrey, "Sugars and Dental Decay", **The Lancet**, 5.2.83.
3. Diet, Nutrition and Health, March 1986, British Medical Association, Report of the Board of Science and Education.
4. Roth, Andrew (1984), **Parliamentary Profiles**, Volume 4.
5. British Sugar Bureau publication, 1983.
6. New Health, January 1984.
7. The Times, 14.5.84.

8. British Medical Association (March 1986), op. cit.
9. British Journal of Nutrition, November 1985.
10. The Guardian, 18.11.85

CHAPTER SEVEN

1. On the basis that it takes 40,000 people to produce 200,000 tonnes of sugar in Jamaica it can be estimated that it will take nearly 12 million people to produce the 58 million tonnes of cane sugar produced by Developing Countries each year. This means that, including their families, around 60 million people are dependent on the industry for a livelihood.
2. Aguilar, F.V. (November 1984), The Making of Cane Sugar: Poverty, Crisis and Change in Negros, Occidental La Salle Monograph Series, No 2, Bacolod City, Philippines. page 98.
3. The Times, 19.9.86.
4. Aguilar, F.V. (November 1984), op. cit., page 98.
5. K.M.P. (1986), Policy Proposals on Agriculture and Countryside Development, KMP, Quezon City, Philippines. Cola Action, Amsterdam, The Netherlands.
6. Oxfam News, Winter 1986.
7. Daily Gleaner, 28.8.86.
8. Weekly Gleaner, 11.11.86.
9. Visit by author to Bernard Lodge Vegetable Farm, February 1986.
10. Workers Time, Vol 12, No 4, July – August 1986.
11. Financial Times, 7.5.86.
12. World Bank News, 10.5.84, "The Sweet Smell of Brazil's Traffic".
13. Financial Times, 7.5.86, "Brazil perseveres with sugar fuel scheme".
14. Folha Sao Paulo, 10.3.87.
15. International Labour Review, January – February, 1983, Vol 122, No 1, pages 111-126.
16. Action for Development, November 1984, "Alcohol to power economic recovery".
17. CULTIVATED AREA OF THE MAIN CROPS IN PERNAMBUCO (1975/82)

CROPS	RATE OF ANNUAL INCREASE (%)
Sugar	+ 4.2
Cotton	− 8.8
Beans	+ 0.4
Manioc, cassava	− 1.5
Maize	− 9.8
Coffee	+ 3.2

F.E.T.A.P.

18. The Rationalisation of the Pernambuco Cane Industry, with the Distribution of Surplus Land to the Rural Workers, reply of the rural workers from the Pernambuco cane growing area, through their Unions FETAP and CONTAG, to a proposal from the employers for a shorter working day with a reduction in pay, FETAP 1983.
19. Frances Rubin, interview with President of CONTAG, The National Federation of Rural Workers, Recife, 16.3.87.
20. Financial Times, 7.5.86.
21. Bueno, Ricardo, 1984, Pro-Alcool: Rumo ao Desastre, Vozes, Petropolis, 4th ed.
22. Silva, Jose Gomes da, Pro-Alcool e Questao Agraria, Cadernos do CEAS, Jan/Feb 1982, p.8 and 9, Salvador BA, Brazil.
23. See Chapter 1.
24. Braga, Ricardo Augusto Pessoa, (1985), A Outra Face do Alcool, Universidade Federal de Pernambuco, Recife PE, Brazil.
25. The Church Commission for Fisherpeople, Brazil Project Numbers 22, 331, 465, 481.
26. Brazil 200.
27. Jornal Ambientalista, Nov/Dec 1986.
28. UNCTAD/TT/61 (14 November 1985), Power Alcohol in Kenya and Zimbabwe: a case study in the transfer of renewable energy technology, Study prepared by Mr David Stuckey and Mr

Calestous Juma in cooperation with the UNCTAD secretariat – United Nations Conference on Trade and Development.

29. Personal interview with Potoya Kuppan, president of the Mauritian Sugar Industry Labourers Union – September 26, 1986.

30. UNCTAD TD/B/C.1/PSC/29/Rev.1 (United Nations, New York, 1984), Studies in the processing, marketing and distribution of commodities, **The processing and marketing of sugar:Areas for international co-operation**, Report by the UNCTAD secretariat.

31. Stevens, C.(ed) (1982), **EEC and the Third World: A Survey 2 – Hunger in the World**, Hodder and Stoughton, in association with the Overseas Development Institute and the Institute of Development Studies.

32. Avramovic, Dragoslav (July 1986), "Depression of Export Commodity Prices", **Third World Quarterly**, Vol 8, No 3.

33. Financial Times, 11.6.86, "Sri Lanka opens $10m sugar complex".

34. Information supplied by the Statistics Division of the Overseas Development Administration, 5.11.86.

35. **To the People of Sri Lanka**, Joint Declaration on the transfer of Lands in Wallassa to foreign companies, printed at Navamga Printers Debiwala, by The Solidarity Committee for the Peasants of Monaragala.

NEW MARKETS FOR SUGAR

1. **New Health**, April 1985.
2. **The Economist**, 10.8.85.
3. Lappe FM, Collins J. (1980), **Food First – The Myth of Scarcity**, Souvenir Press, London, page 234.
4. **New Internationalist**, May 1984.
5. Sheiham, Aubrey (1983), "Dental Caries in Underdeveloped Countries", **Cariology Today**, Int Congr, Zurich. pp33-39.
6. Konsumo Dabaw – Project Number Philippines 42.

CHAPTER EIGHT

1. This is in line with the proposal that the Commission put forward for setting quotas, in 1974.
2. Harris, Simon (December 1985), **Review of the EC Sugar Market**, Report for the World Bank, Washington DC, USA, BSD Ltd, page 78.
3. Ibid, page 82.
4. Ibid, page 73.
5. Ibid, page 74.
6. The following countries were members of the International Sugar Agreement in 1985:

Exporting Members

Argentina, Australia, Austria, Barbados, Belize, Bolivia, Brazil, Colombia, Congo, Costa Rica, Cuba, Dominican Republic, Ecuador, El Salvador, EC, Fiji, Guatemala, Guyana, Haiti, Honduras, Hungary, India, Ivory Coast, Jamaica, Madagascar, Malawi, Mauritius, Mexico, Nicaragua, Pakistan, Panama, Papua New Guinea, Paraguay, Peru, Philippines, St Christopher-Nevis, South Africa, Swaziland, Thailand, Trinidad and Tobago, Uganda, Zimbabwe.

Importing Members

Canada, Arab Republic of Egypt, Finland, German Democratic Republic, Iraq, Japan, Republic of Korea, Norway, Sweden, Union of Soviet Socialist Republics, United States of America.

(Sugar Year Book, 1985)

7. Gordon-Ashworth, F. (1985), **International Commodity Control – A Contemporary History**, Croom Helm Ltd, page 178.
8. FAO Economic and Social Development Paper, 50. **Sugar: Major Trade and Stabilisation Issues in the Eighties**, Food and Agricultural Organisation of the United Nations, Rome 1985, para 30.
9. Ibid, para 3.
10. Gordon-Ashworth, F.(1985), op. cit., page 181.